Virginia Colonial Militia

Virginia County Records

VOLUME II

VIRGINIA COLONIAL MILITIA
1651-1776

EDITED BY

William Armstrong Crozier

CLEARFIELD

Reprinted for
Clearfield Company, Inc. by
Genealogical Publishing Co., Inc.
Baltimore, Maryland
2000, 2004

Originally published as Volume II
of *Virginia County Records*
New York, 1905
Reprinted: Southern Book Company
Baltimore, 1954
Reissued: Genealogical Publishing Co., Inc.
Baltimore, 1965, 1973, 1982, 1986
Library of Congress Catalogue Card Number 67-29835
International Standard Book Number 0-8063-0566-5
Made in the United States of America

Virginia

Colonial Militia

1651 - 1776

EDITED BY

William Armstrong Crozier

*Editor of Crozier's American Armory; The Use and Abuse of
Coat Armor in America; Records of Spotsylvania County,
Virginia; History of the Buckner Family, etc., etc.*

MEMBER OF

*British Record Society, Historical Society of Pennsylvania,
Virginia Historical Society, Topsfield Historical
Society, New York Genealogical and
Biographical Society,
Corresponding Member of the
Old North West Genealogical Society.*

PUBLISHED BY

THE GENEALOGICAL ASSOCIATION

NEW YORK   MDCCCCV

OR many years past, and especially since the establishment of the various Patriotic Societies, research amongst the records of Colonial Virginia has been fraught with many obstacles, the most important being the destruction of county records. This, of course, is irremediable. The second difficulty is the fact, that all printed data on the subject is contained in many volumes and pamphlets, which can only be found in a few of the largest libraries.

Knowing, from personal experience, the great value of a work that would contain, in one or two volumes, not only the best of what has already appeared, but new material as well, I have hesitated to attempt that which so many others were more eminently qualified to perform. Finding, however, that patience was not in this case bringing its own reward, I have taken the initiative, and, while fully conscious of its many shortcomings, have placed before the public this initial volume of data relative to the Virginia Colonial Militia.

I would refer those who may be desirous of studying *in extenso* Lord Dunmore's War—the participants in which, on the Colonial side, were soon to turn their military experience against the mother country—to the "Documentary History of Dunmore's War," so ably edited by Reuben Gold Thwaites, LL.D.

WM. ARMSTRONG CROZIER

209 West 84th Street
    New York City
November 1, 1905

Contents

Land Bounty Certificates

FOR SERVICE IN THE FRENCH AND INDIAN WARS.

For participation in the wars of the Colony of Virginia against the French and Indians, and for service rendered by the Militia in defence of the frontiers, the King's Proclamation of 1763 granted certain amounts of land.

The amount given to field officers was 5,000 acres ; to captains, 3,000 acres ; to subalterns or staff officers, 2,000 acres ; to non-commissioned officers, 200 acres ; to privates, 50 acres.

The Original Warrants or Certificates of the subjoined abstracts are to be found in two MMS. Volumes, deposited in the State Land Office, Richmond, Va.

The original spelling of proper and Christian names has been strictly adhered to. It has not been thought necessary to print the original Proclamation of 1763, which may be found in Hening's Statutes at Large of Virginia, Vol. VII., Appendix.

CERTIFICATES.

Alexr. Fowler, as assignee to Lieut. George Brooke ; served in Capt. Marcus Rankin's Company, under command of Major Gen. Sir John Irwin, Col. of His Majesty's late 74th Regt. of Foot. At Court held for Yohogania Co., Mar. 24, 1780.

Alexr. Fowler, assignee of Lieut. Henry Dalway, who served in Capt. Alexr. Rigby's Co., under command of Sir John Irwin, etc., 74th Regt. of Foot. Yohogania Co., Mar. 24, 1780.

John Fleming served as Lieut. in Col. Francis' Battalion of Penna. troops in Capt. Kern's company of Light Horse. Monongalia Co. Court, Mar. 14, 1780.

Discharge from Adam Stephen, Col. in the Va. Regt., to James Roe, soldier in Capt. Mordecai Buckner's company of Va. At Fort Lewis, Feb. 23, 1762.

Doctor Thomas Lloyd, engaged in company of Rangers in July, 1755, under command of Capt. Wm. Preston, and served until company was disbanded in June, 1756 ; acting as surgeon to that and other companies, etc. ; engaged a second time in company of Rangers under Preston, June, 1757, and continued therein on the frontiers of Augusta until May, 1759, when company was disbanded ; acting as surgeon in said company and the neigh-

boring companies of Rangers in garrison, etc., all without pay.   Botetourt
Co. Court, 1780.

Alexr. Fowler, Lieut. in Capt. Hy. Peyton's company under command
of Major Gen. Sir John Irwin, commanding 74th Regt. of Foot in America,
from 1758 to Dec. 7, 1763.   Yohogania Co. Court, Mar. 24, 1780.

Jno. Nash, Sergt. seven and one-half years in Capt. Hy. Woodward's
company, Col. Washington's Regt. in the last French war.   Cumberland Co.
Court, Mar. 27, 1780.

Jno. Vachob, soldier in Capt. Wm. Preston's company of Rangers in the
late war, Great Britain and France, 1758.   Augusta Co. Court, Mar. 21, 1780.

John Davis, Sergt. in Capt. Wm. Preston's company of Rangers in 1758.
Greenbrier Co. Court, May 17, 1780.

Wm. Evans, artificer in a detachment of the Royal train of Artillery
commanded by Capt. David Hays in America, from 1758 to 1760.   Yohogania
Co. Court, Mar. 24, 1780.

Wm. Maxey, soldier in the last Indian war in 1760, served 6 months
under Capt. James Gunn.   Buckingham Co. Court, Nov. 8, 1779.

Wm. Long, Lieut. in Virginia service entitled to 2,000 acres of land, and
desires to locate same in Western Waters in Fincastle Co.   (Signed) Dunmore, Jan. 31, 1774.

Essex to wit.   John Baughan made oath that his brother James Baughan
served as a soldier in the last war in a regiment raised for immediate defense
of the state "above twenty years ago, until same was disbanded."

John Stuart, assignee and administrator of Joseph Donnelson, deceased,
made oath that said Donnelson served as Ensign in 1st Virginia Regiment,
commanded by Wm. Byrd, until same was disbanded.   Greenbrier Co. Court,
Mar. 22, 1783.

Wm. Preston, Captain of a company of Rangers raised by Act of Assembly, from July 14, 1755, to June 24, 1756, under command of Col. James
Patton, until he (Patton) was killed in the service, and then under immediate
command of the Governor, and the remainder of the time under command
of James Lewis, an officer of the Virginia regiment.   Wm. Preston commanded another company of Rangers raised by Act of Assembly of June 8,
1757, when his commission was dated, and continued in the service until May
4, 1759, when company was disbanded.   Montgomery Co. Court, April 5, 1780.

Wm. Preston is representative of the following persons, who served in
the above mentioned company of Rangers, to wit : Josiah Cummings, a corporal ; Thomas Saunders, a drummer ; Solly Mulliear, James Hulman, Moses
Fisher, Gardner Adkins and Nicho. Smith, privates.

Bond Estle, soldier in Capt. Wm. Preston's company of Rangers, 1758.
Greenbrier Co. Court, Feb. 15, 1780.

Thos. Galbreath, soldier in Capt. Peter Hogg's company of Rangers in
the year 1758.   Augusta Co. Court, Nov. 10, 1779.

James Colquhond, soldier in 2nd Virginia Regiment, Col. Byrd, till properly discharged in 1750.   Caroline Co. Court, 1780.

Edmund Wagner, deceased, a subaltern in the Virginia Regiment, entitled to 2,000 acres of land. Andrew Wagner is his heir. March 7, 1774. (Signed) Dunmore, Govr.

Henry Dawson, soldier in a Virginia regiment in 1760 and served through the campaign under command of the late Col. Wm. Byrd. Amherst Co. Court, March, 1780.

John Jones, Ensign in Col. Thomson's Penna. Regiment, Indian war about 1757, in which capacity he served through the whole war. Frederick Co. Court, July 4, 1780.

James Anderson, Captain in Col. John Johnston's New Jersey Regiment in 1756, in which capacity he served until regiment was disbanded. Frederick Co. Court, Mar. 8, 1780.

Wm. Daingerfield, Captain in Col. Byrd's Virginia Regiment till disbanded. Afterwards in regiment commanded by Col. Adam Stephen. Spotsylvania Co. Court, June 15, 1780.

Thos. Patterson, assignee of Thomas Ealey, a soldier in war between Great Britain and France. Yohogania Co. Court, May, 1780.

Wm. Christy, Ensign in 1st Bat. of Penna. troops 1760, under command of Capt. Saml. West, in Col. Byrd's regiment, and then legally discharged. Yohogania Co. Court, March, 1780.

Alexr. Fowler, assignee of Lieut. Butler Stubbs, who served in last war in America in Capt. George Berkeley's company, under command of Major Gen. Sir John Irwin, Col. of His Majesty's late 74th Regiment of Foot. Yohogania Co., Mar. 24, 1780.

Alexr. Fowler, assignee of Lieut. Angus MacNeill, who served in Capt. George Berkeley's company, under command of Sir John Irwin, Col. of 74th Regiment of Foot in the last war in America. Yohogania Co., Mar. 24, 1780.

Benj. Temple, entitled to 2,000 acres of land, agreeable to His Majesty's Proclamation in the year 1763. Nov. 27, 1774. (Signed) Dunmore, Govr.

Holt Richardson, Gent., proved before the Court that Col. Wm. Peachey was Paymaster of the 2nd Virginia Regiment in 1758. King William Co. Court, Nov. 18, 1779.

Holt Richardson, Gent., proved that Thomas Elliott, Gent., was Paymaster to Col. Wm. Peachey's Batt. in the year 1759 and part of 1760. King William Co. Court, Nov. 18, 1779.

William Alexander, allowed 200 acres for serving as a non-commissioned officer in Col. Byrd's 2nd Virginia Regiment. Rockbridge Court, Nov., 1779.

William Morriss, Lieut. in the late war between Great Britain, France and the Indians. Goochland Co. Court, Sept., 1779.

Archibald Thompson, entitled to 200 acres of land for military service as under the King's Proclamation in the year 1763. Montgomery Court, Nov., 1779.

Capt. William Russell, entitled to 3,000 acres of land agreeable to the King's Proclamation in the year 1763. Dunmore, Govr.

Thomas Mastin, entitled to 50 acres of land under the King's Proclamation of 1763. Montgomery Court, Nov., 1779.

Robert Miller, entitled to 50 acres of land under Proclamation of 1763, for military services. Montgomery Court, Oct., 1779.

Samuel Newberry, entitled to 50 acres of land under Proclamation of 1763, for military services. Montgomery Court, Nov., 1779.

William Hughes made oath that Matthew Roberts served in the 1st Virginia Regiment under Col. Byrd, as a soldier. James City Co., Nov. 8, 1779.

Matthew Riddle, soldier in the 2nd Virginia Regiment of regulars, raised within the then Colony, now Commonwealth of Virginia, according to the King's Proclamation of Oct. 7, 1763. Henrico Co. Court, Sept. 5, 1779.

John Stanley and Thomas Green, Jr., who made oath that they were soldiers in the 2nd and last regiment of regulars raised in Virginia in the war between Great Britain and France. Hanover Co. Court, Sept. 2, 1779.

David Poe and Simon Gillett served in the 1st Virginia Regiment in the last war as soldiers under command of Col. Wm. Byrd. James City Co., Nov. 8, 1779.

Samuel Campbell served as a soldier in Capt. Wm. Preston's company of Rangers in 1758, until he was discharged. Greenbrier Co., Feb. 15, 1780.

Francis Amos, served in the last French war on the Virginia frontier, one year as corporal under Capt. Fleming, and one year as corporal under Capt. Charles Scott in Col. Peachey's Regiment. Buckingham Co., Nov. 8, 1779.

John Fulton, allowed 50 acres for services as a soldier in Capt. John Dickenson's Company of Rangers in late war between Great Britain and France. Augusta Co., Mar. 21, 1780.

William McGehee enlisted and served in Capt. Wm. Phillip's company of Volunteer Rangers in 1763, until legally discharged. Louisa County, March 13, 1780.

William Duncan, soldier in Capt. Lewis's company of Regulars in last war. Botetourt Court, March, 1780.

Jacob Gooding, Captain in a corps of Rangers in 1758, under the immediate command of Col. (now Gen.) Washington. Fairfax Co., July, 1780.

John Baller, Sergt. in Capt. Dickinson's company of Rangers on the frontiers of the Colony, 1756 and 1757. Botetourt Co., Feb., 1780.

Jacob Crosthwait, soldier in Col. Byrd's Regiment in 1758. Orange Co., Aug. 26, 1779.

John Wooton, soldier under Capt. James Gunn in 1st Virginia Regiment commanded by Col. Wm. Byrd in last war. Halifax Co., May 18, 1780.

Joseph Wooton, soldier in 2nd Virginia Regiment under Capt. Gabriel Throckmorton in 1760 and 1761. Halifax Co., Apr. 21, 1780.

Archibald Alexander, deceased, Capt. of a Company of Volunteers and marched them to Greenbrier in order to proceed against the Shawnees in the year 1757, and William Alexander is his heir-at-law. Botetourt Co. Court, Aug. 10, 1780.

Wm. Dounaway, soldier from 1759 to 1762 in Virginia Regiments and was legally discharged. Bedford Court, Jan., 1780.

Archibald Lamb, soldier, 1759-1762 in the Va. Regts, and was legally discharged. Bedford Court, Jan., 1780.

John Penix, soldier in Capt. Overton's Company of Rangers in 1756 till legally discharged. Louisa County, March 13, 1780.

John Johnston, soldier in a ranging company under Capt. Wm. Preston. Washington Co., March 21, 1780.

Edward Harris, soldier in Capt. Meredith's Company of Rangers in the year 1760 until legally discharged. Louisa County, March 13, 1780.

John Shields, soldier in Capt. John Dickinson's Company of Rangers in the year 1759 in the late war between Great Britain and France. Augusta County, March 21, 1780.

William Shields, soldier in Capt. John Dickinson's Company of Rangers in the year 1759. Augusta County, March 21, 1780.

Samuel Meredith, Gent., who served in the late war between Great Britain and France as Captain, certifies, that John Hodges, deceased, served in the said war as Serg. in the 2nd Virginia Regiment under command of Col. Wm. Byrd, until legally discharged. Martha Hodges, relict and administratrix.

Doctor Thomas Walker served as Commissary-General seven years to the British and Colonial troops in the last war. Botetourt County, Aug. 10, 1780.

Richard Burke, heir at law to Thos. Burke a soldier about twenty years ago in one of the regiments raised for the immediate defense of this state. Essex Co. Court, Feb., 1780.

Philemon Hawkins, a native of Virginia, soldier in Regiment commanded by the late Col. Wm. Byrd in the late war between Great Britain and France. Prince Edward Co. Court, April, 1780.

Joseph Webster, a soldier under Capt. James Gunn in Col. Wm. Byrd's Regiment in the year 1760. Henry County, May 25, 1780.

Joseph Bradberry, soldier under Capt. John Lightfoot in Col. Byrd's Regiment in 1760. Henry County, May 25, 1780.

Amos Evans, a soldier under Capt. James Gunn in Col. Wm. Byrd's Regiment in the year 1760. Henry County, May 25, 1780.

Thomas Hayle, non-commissioned officer in or about the year 1754 in the 1st Virginia Regiment in an expedition against the Indians. Frederick County, April 11, 1780.

John Trigg, Sergeant under command of Gen. Washington in the 1st Virginia Regiment until same was disbanded. Berkeley Court, August, 1780.

John Montgomery, soldier in Capt. Chas. Lewis' company of Rangers in the year 1758, in the war between Great Britain and France. Augusta County, Feb. 15, 1780.

Christopher Fry, non-commissioned officer in the old Virginia Regiment, in which capacity he served until the Regiment was disbanded. Frederick County, March 8, 1780.

Saml. Poe, Sergeant in the 1st Virginia Regiment and entitled to 200 acres of land under Proc. of 1763. Williamsburg, May 22, 1774. Dunmore (Govr.)

George Vaughan, soldier under Capt. John Lightfoot in a regular corps raised in the state in 1758 against Fort Du Quesne. Halifax County, March 16, 1780.

John Reynolds, soldier in old Virginia Regiment during late war. Frederick County, May 2, 1780.

Augustine White, soldier in each of the old Virginia Regiments commanded by Col. Byrd and Col. Stephen in the late war, until they were disbanded ; and that he was a non-commissioned officer. Frederick County, May 2, 1780.

Colonel John Gibson (a Justice of this county) served as a Deputy Commissary in the late war between Great Britain and France. Yohogania Co. Set Court, Feb., 1780.

Bartlet Ellis, Sergeant in Va. Bat. of Regulars commanded by Col. Wm. Byrd in 1755. Richard Ellis made oath that Bartlet Ellis, together with himself, listed under Capt. Saml. Meredith in the late French and Indian war with Great Britain, and that the said Bartlet acted as Sergeant sometime after his enlistment, and continued to act as such until the expiration of the time for which they were enlisted. Hanover County Court, April 6, 1780.

John Savage, entitled to 3,000 acres of land agreeable to the King's Proclamation in the year 1763. Feb. 24, 1774. Dunmore (Govr.)

Thomas Taylor, heir-at-law to Geo. Taylor, Jnr., deceased, entitled to 2,000 acres of land for said George's service in the last war, agreeable to His Majesty's Proclamation of 1763. Williamsburg, Feb. 12, 1774. Dunmore.

Francis Gibbs, soldier in Capt. Hogg's company of Rangers until duly discharged in 1758. Orange Co., May 25, 1780.

Richard Vernon in the years 1755, 1756, 1757, 1758, and 1759 acted as a wagon master, forage master and assistant commissary to the troops under the command of Genls. Braddock, Forbes and Stanwix upon their several expeditions, and particularly superintended the wagons belonging to the Colony of Virginia. Culpeper Co. Court, May 16, 1780.

Edwd. Sprigg, who is and has been a resident of this state 8 years, proved that his father, Edward Sprigg, served as Capt. in the requirement (Regt. ?) commanded by Geo. Washington, Esqr., and lost his life in the service ; and that he is heir-at-law, etc. Prince William Co., July 3, 1780.

William Dempsey, a soldier in Capt. Smith's Regular Co. last war till it was disbanded. Botetourt Co. Court, March, 1780.

Thos. Casady, decd., soldier in old Va. Regt. last war, Col. Washington, Commander, until legally discharged. Thos. Cassaday heir at law. Botetourt Co. Court, Feby., 1780.

David Galloway, Jnr., soldier in Capt. Dickinson's company of Rangers in last war, till legally discharged. Botetourt Co. Court, Feby., 1780.

Francis Eppes, Lieut. 2d Va. Regt. last war. (Signed) W. Byrd, May 20, 1774.

Wm. Mann, deceased, Sergt. in Col. Peachey's Batt. in 1759. Moses Mann, eldest son and heir. Botetourt Co. Court, Feby., 1780.

Humphrey Madison, deceased, Ensign in Capt. Dickinson's Co. of Rangers in 1756, and lost his life in the service of his country. Catherine Arbuckle, wife of Wm. Arbuckle and heiress at law of Humphrey Madison, deceased. Botetourt Co. Court, Decr., 1780.

Wm. Smith, soldier in Capt. Hogg's company of Rangers until duly discharged in 1758. Orange Co. Court, May 25, 1780.

Wm. Watson, served his enlistment as a regular soldier in Capt. Overton's company of Regulars before the year 1763. Orange Co. Court, Mar. 23, 1780.

Jas. McCutchin, soldier under Capt. John Blagge in Col. Byrd's Regt. in 1760. Henry Co. Court, May 25, 1780.

David Lyle, Sergt. in 2d Va. Regt., Col. Wm. Byrd commanding. King William Co., April Court, 1780.

John King, soldier in 2d Va. Regt., Col. Wm. Byrd commanding, until disbanded. King William Co., April 20, 1780.

Geo. Stubblefield, Gent., Cadet in Adam Stephen's Regt. raised for defense of this state. Spotsylvania Co. Court, June, 1780.

Jno. Fitzjarrell, Sergt. in Va. Regt. commanded by Col. Wm. Byrd in 1759 and 1760. Amherst Co. Court, Feby., 1780.

William Camp, William King and James Lankford each knew that the other served as volunteer soldiers under Capt. Christopher Hudson in the year 1758, in war between Great Britain and France, said Camp as Corporal, and the other two as common soldiers. Hanover Co., June 1, 1780.

Wm. Thorp, native of Virginia, Sergt. 1755-1762 in the late French war. Certificate signed by Chas. Scott, Brig.-Genl., that he was then regularly discharged. Bedford Court, Dec., 1779.

John Thorp, deceased, regular soldier under Genl. Forbes in 1758, and then departed this life. Wm. Thorp, a native of Virginia and heir-at-law of John Thorp, deceased. Bedford Court, Jany., 1780.

Thos. Thorp, Corporal in the late French war, 1759-1762. Bedford Court, Jany., 1780.

Richard Timberlake, native of Virginia, soldier for six months under Gen. Forbes in 1758, in the late French war. Bedford Court, May, 1780.

James Baker, Gent., deceased, Lieut. 1st Va. Regt. of Regulars, commanded by Col. Geo. Washington, in 1758, and died in the service. Proved by Wm. Hughes, Hustings Court of Williamsburg, Feb. 9. 1780. Lawrence Baker, Gent., heir-at-law to the said James Baker, Gent., deceased. Surry Co. Court, April 25, 1780.

Edgcomb G. Williams, soldier under Capt. Nath. Gist in Col. Adam Stephen's Regt. in 1762. Henry Co., May 25, 1780.

John McKensie, Sergt. in 1st Va. Regt. until reduction of same, when he was regularly discharged. Kentucky Co., Nov. 2, 1780.

John Miller, soldier in Capt. Wm. Preston's company of Rangers in 1758 and 1759, and continued in said company until they were discharged. Greenbrier Co., March 22, 1780.

James Johnston, soldier in Capt. Dickerson's company of Rangers, in which he remained until discharged in 1759. Greenbrier Co. Court, March, 1780.

John Jameson, soldier in Maj. Robert Stewart's company of 1st Va. Regt. Proved by John Estle, assignee of John Jameson. Greenbrier Court, Feb. 13, 1780.

Ben Lohone, entitled to 50 acres for services in last war, agreeable to proclamation of 1763. Feb. 22, 1774. Dunmore.

John Estle, soldier in Capt. Wm. Preston's company of Rangers in r758. Greenbrier Co., Feb. 15, 1780.

James Roe, soldier in 1st Va. Regt. Discharge dated Feb., 1762, from Col. Adam Stephen of the 2d Regt. Southampton Co., May 11, 1780.

Pharel McFaddin, soldier in Col. Peachey's Va. Regt., or Frontier Bat. Buckingham Co., Nov. 8, 1779.

James Burnett, soldier in Col. Peachey's Va. Regt., or Frontier Bat. Buckingham Co., Nov. 8, 1779.

Martin Webb, soldier six months in Col. Peachey's Regt., or Frontier Bat. Buckingham Co., Nov. 8, 1779.

Richard Baldock, deceased, Sergt. in a Regt. under the command of the then Col. Stephen in the late war between Great Britain, France and Spain. Levy Baldock, heir-at-law to the said Richard Baldock, deceased. Amherst Co. Court, Feb., 1780.

Levy Baldock, soldier in Va. Regt. under command of the late Col. Wm. Byrd in the late war between Great Britain, France and Spain. Amherst Co., Feb. Court, 1780.

Frederick Fitzgerald, soldier in Capt. Wm. Preston's company of Rangers in 1762. Henry Co., May 25, 1780.

Thomas Kinkead, soldier in Capt. Wm. Preston's company of Rangers in 1758 and 1759. Greenbrier Co., March 21, 1780.

John Hodges, Gent., is due 2,000 acres of land under the King's Proclamation, for the services of a certain Francis Eppes during the last French wars, who was a Lieut. in 2d Va. Regt., and which said Eppes hath assigned to said Hodges. Prince William Co. Court, June 5, 1780.

William Gooch, Sergt. in late war, is entitled to 200 acres under the King's Proclamation of 1763. May 7, 1774. Dunmore.

William Blanton, Sergt. in 1st Va. Regt. until discharged. Greenbrier Co., Feb. 15, 1780.

Edward McMullin, soldier in Capt. Dickerson's company of Rangers on the Frontier in 1758 and 1759. Botetourt Court, Feb., 1780.

Thomas Kelly, Corp. in Capt. Dickerson's company of Rangers in 1757, 1758 and 1759. Botetourt Court, Feb., 1780.

John McMullin, soldier in Capt. Dickerson's company of Rangers in 1758 and 1759. Botetourt Court, Feb., 1780.

Robt. Gillespie, Senr., Sergt. in Capt. Dickerson's company of Rangers in the year 1754. Botetourt Court, Feb., 1780.

Thos. Carpenter, soldier in Capt. Dickerson's company of Rangers in 1759. Botetourt Court, Feb., 1780.

Jacob Parsinger, Senr., proved to this Court that he and his two sons, Abraham and Phillip, who died under age, each served in Capt. Dickerson's company of Rangers in 1757. Botetourt Court, Feb., 1780.

Patrick Carrigan, soldier in Capt. Dickerson's company of Rangers in 1758. Botetourt Court, Feb., 1780.

Wm. Crayton, entitled to 50 acres of land under the King's Proclamation of 1763. Jan. 22, 1774. Dunmore.

Thos. Elliott, Lieut. in Va. Bat. of Regulars, commanded by Wm. Peachey, Esqr., in 1759. King William Co. Court, Jan., 1780.

James Hilling, soldier in Capt. Thos. Booth's Co. 2d Va. Regt., commanded by Col. Wm. Byrd, deceased, and served therein till said Regt. was disbanded before 1763. Hustings Court for Williamsburg, Feb. 7, 1780.

Arthur Campbell, entitled to 2,000 acres of land for services in last war, agreeable to King's Proclamation of 1763. Dec. 15, 1773. Dunmore.

Henry Harrison, son and heir of Capt. Henry Harrison, deceased, is entitled to 3,000 acres of land, agreeable to the King's Proclamation of 1763. Dec. 31, 1773. Dunmore.

Richard Hickman, deceased, Lieut. in the Va. Regt. of Regulars commanded by Adam Stephen, Esqr., in the year 1763, and continued in said office until said Regt. was disbanded. James Hickman, brother and heir-at-law. King William County, Jan. 20, 1780.

Wm. Fleming, assistant surgeon by appointment from Gov. Dinwiddie, 1755, in 1st Va. Regt. until reduction thereof in 1762. Kentucky Co., Nov. 2, 1779.

Thos. Lovett, Drummer in the Va. Regt, 1754, until reduction thereof in 1762. Kentucky Co., Nov. 2, 1779.

James Hill, entitled to 200 acres of land, agreeable to the King's Proclamation of 1763. March 1, 1774. Dunmore.

James Hebdon, entitled to 50 acres of land, agreeable to the King's Proclamation of 1763. April 21, 1774. Dunmore.

John Anderson, Sergt. in 2d Va. Regt. commanded by Hon. Wm. Byrd, Esqr., agreeable to King's Proclamation of October, 1763. May 7, 1774. Dunmore.

Joel Harlow, soldier in late war, entitled to 50 acres of land, agreeable to proclamation of the King in 1763. April 23, 1774. Dunmore.

Nicholas Sallis (or Sallaie), soldier in Va. Regt. late war. Certificate signed by Andrew Lewis. (No date.)

Jno. Murray, deceased, Ensign in Capt. Alex. McClenachan's company of Independents on the expedition against the Indians, commanded by Col. Bouquet in 1764. Mrs. Elizabeth Murray, widow and heir of Dr. John Murray, deceased. Augusta Co. Court, Dec. 21, 1779.

Thomas McGregor, soldier in Capt. Wm. Preston's company of Rangers. Augusta Co. Court, Nov. 18, 1779.

James Dunlap, deceased, Lieut. in Capt. Peter Hogg's company of Rangers, and was destroyed by the enemy, French and Indians, at the fort in the upper tract on the south branch of the Potomac, in the year 1758. James Brown and Adam Gutherey, nephews and heirs-at-law of said James Dunlap, deceased. Augusta Co. Court, Dec. 21, 1779.

Thos. Scott, soldier in a ranging company against the Indians in 1764. Augusta Co. Court, Nov. 17, 1779.

Jno. Clark, Sergt. in a ranging company against the Indians in 1764. Augusta Co., Nov. 17, 1779.

James McMahon, soldier in Capt. Hogg's company of Rangers. Augusta Co., Nov. 17, 1779.

Chas. Lewis, deceased, Lieut. in Capt. Preston's company of Rangers. Capt. in company of Independents on the expedition against the Indians, commanded by Col. Bouquet in 1764. Augusta Co., Nov. 17, 1779.

Henry Pigg, private in 2d Va. Regt. of Regulars in late war between Great Britain and France. Prince Edward Co., Jan. 17, 1780.

Richard Foster, private in Capt. Saml. Overton's company of volunteers in the late war between Great Britain and France. Prince Edward Co., Jan. 17, 1780.

Jos. Truman, private in Capt. Obediah Woodson's company of Volunteers in late war. Prince Edward Co., Jan., 1780.

Alexr. Le Grand, Sergt. in company of Volunteers in late war between Great Britain and France. Prince Edward Co., Jan., 1780.

Jno. Morton, Gent., Lieut. in a company of Volunteers in the late war; by order from Gov. Dinwiddie joined Maj. Andrew Lewis' detachment from 1st Va. Regt. of Regulars, and continued in the service six months. Prince Edward Co., Jan. 17, 1780.

Thos. Morton, 2d Lieut. in company of Volunteers in late war between Great Britain and France, and by order joined Maj. Andrew Lewis' detachment of Regulars from 1st Va. Regt., and continued in service six months. Prince Edward Co., Jan 17, 1780.

Chas. Croucher, soldier in Col. Adam Stephen's Va. Regt. until disbanded. Hustings Court of Williamsburg, Feb. 7, 1780.

Sylvester Hughes, soldier in Capt. Robt, Stewart's company of Regulars, Col. Wm. Byrd's 2d Va. Regt., and continued therein until disbanded. Williamsburg, Hustings Court, Feb. 7, 1780.

Edwd. Cary, entitled to 2,000 acres, agreeable to proclamation of 1763. Williamsburg, Nov. 22, 1773. : Dunmore.

Morris Evington, entitled to 200 acres of land, agreeable to His Majesty's Proclamation of 1763. Williamsburg, Jan. 3, 1774. Dunmore.

Francis Scott, entitled to 50 acres of land, agreeable to His Majesty's Proclamation of 1763. Jan. 31, 1774. Dunmore.

Wm. Henderson, soldier in Capt. Alexr. McClenachan's company of Independents on the expedition against the Indians, commanded by Col. Bouquet, in 1764. Augusta Co., Nov. 19, 1779.

Wm. Kinkiad, soldier in Capt. Chas. Lewis' company on the expedition against the Indians, commanded by Col. Bouquet in 1763. Augusta Co., Jan. 18, 1783.

Wm. Hughes, Lieut. and Adjutant in Col. Adam Stephen's Va. Regt. in the year 1762, and served until Regt. was disbanded. Williamsburg, Feb. 9, 1780.

James Ritchey, soldier in Capt. Christian's company of Rangers on the Cherokee expedition, commanded by Col. Wm. Byrd in 1760. Botetourt Court, Dec., 1779.

Saml. French, Sergt. in the late war, entitled to 200 acres, agreeable to His Majesty's Proclamation of 1763. Williamsburg, May 29, 1774. Dunmore.

Geo. Muse, Lieut. Col. (until properly discharged) in a Regt. raised for immediate defense of this state in 1754. Caroline Co. Court, Feb., 1780.

Thos. Ayres, Sergt. in 1758 (till properly discharged) in a Regt. raised for the immediate defense of this state. Caroline Co., Feb. 10, 1780.

Anthony Kenty, soldier in Capt. Saml. Meredith's company of Rangers in 1760 until legally discharged. Proved by Wm. Melton. Louisa Co., Feb. 14, 1780.

Chas. Jenkins, soldier in Capt. Saml. Overton's company of Rangers in 1756, till legally discharged. Louisa Co., Feb. 14, 1780.

Wm. Speere, soldier in late war between Great Britain and France, and remained with his regt. until disbanded. Certificate signed by Saml. Meredith. King William Co., Feb. 16, 1780.

James Ratliff, soldier in Capt. Saml. Overton's company of Rangers in 1755. Louisa Co., Feb. 14, 1780.

Geo. Sims, soldier in Capt. Saml. Overton's company of Rangers in 1755. Louisa Co., Feb. 14, 1780.

Andrew Jameson, soldier under Capt. John Dickinson in 1758 in a ranging company. Kentucky Court, Nov. 2, 1779.

Thos. Moss, Drummer in a Regt. raised for the immediate defense of this state in 1754. Caroline Court, Feb., 1780.

John McDonald, soldier in a Regiment raised for the immediate defense of this state in 1760. Caroline Court, Feb., 1780.

Jno. Harvey, soldier (till properly discharged), in 1758, in a Regt. raised for immediate defense of the state.

Christopher Blackburn, Sergt. in the last French war in 1754. Caroline Co., Feb. 10, 1780.

Joseph Gatewood, soldier in 1st Va. Regt. commanded by Col. Geo. Washington, and continued in said service till Regt. was disbanded. Essex Co., Feb. 21, 1780.

Wm. Kernal, soldier during last war between Great Britain and France, above 20 years ago, in a Regt. commanded by Wm. Byrd, raised for immediate defense of the colony. Essex Co., Feb. 21, 1780.

Jno. Letcher, soldier in a corps raised for the defense of Va., and commanded by Geo. Washington, etc. Lucy Morton, widow of John Letcher, his heiress. Essex Co., Feb. 21, 1780.

Wm. Morton, soldier in Capt. Daingerfield's company, discharged from the Va. Regt., he having the dropsy, being unfitted for the service. (Signed) Fredericksburg, July, 1763. Adam Stephen.

Richd. Chapman, soldier in the Va. Regt. commanded by Col. Wm Byrd, entitled to 50 acres of land, agreeable to the King's Proclamation of 1763. Washington Co., Jan. 18, 1780.

Francis Farmer, soldier in a Va. Regt. commanded by Hon. Wm. Byrd, entitled to 50 acres of land, agreeable to the King's Proclamation of 1763. Washington Co., Jan. 18, 1780.

Henry Dooly, soldier in Va. Regt. under command of late Wm. Byrd, Esqr., entitled to 50 acres of land, agreeable to King's Proclamation of 1763.

Arthur Campbell, assignee of John Donnelly, who served as a non-commissioned officer in the Va. Regt. commanded by Col. Wm. Byrd, and entitled to 200 acres of land under proclamation of 1763. Washington Co., Jan. 18, 1780.

Arthur Campbell, assignee of Drury Pickett, who was a non-commissioned officer in the Va. regiment commanded by Col. Wm. Byrd, and entitled to 200 acres of land under proclamation of 1763. Washington Co., Jan. 18, 1780.

Arthur Campbell, assignee of Thos. Bromley, who was a soldier in Col. Wm. Byrd's regiment, entitled to 50 acres of land under proclamation of 1763. Washington Co., Jan. 18, 1780.

Arthur Campbell, assignee of Richard Staunton, who was a non-commissioned officer in Col. Wm. Byrd's Regt., entitled to 50 acres of land under proclamation of 1763. Washington Co., Jan. 18, 1780.

Arthur Campbell, assignee of Jno. Semmon, who was a soldier in Col. Wm. Byrd's Va. Regt., entitled to 50 acres of land under proclamation of 1763. Washington Co., Jan. 18, 1780.

Wm. Baker, Sergt. 1st Va. Regt., commanded by Col. Geo. Washington, and continued in service until Regt. was disbanded. Proved by John Hickman, Gent. King William Co., Feb. 17, 1780.

Edward Goldman, Ensign, 2d Va. Regt. raised for immediate defense, etc., until properly discharged. Spotsylvania Co., Feb. 17, 1780.

Richard Goldman, Christopher Key and Thos. Samuel made oath that Thos. Goldman is elder brother of within named Edward Goldman, and always understood that the said Thomas is heir-at-law to the said Edward Goldman, deceased. Caroline Co., Feb. 19, 1780.

Reuben Munday, soldier, in 1760, till properly discharged, in Regt. raised for immediate defense of this state. Caroline Co., Feb. 10, 1780.

Edward Sutton, soldier, in 1760, in 1st Va. Regt. raised for immediate defense of the state. Spotsylvania Co., Feb. 17, 1780.

Bartlett Goodman, soldier in Capt. Throgmorton's company of Rangers in 1759, till properly discharged. Louisa Co., Feb. 14, 1780.

Capt. Wm. Phillips, makes oath that John Gilbert served in his company of Volunteer Rangers till legally discharged in 1763. The said Capt. Phillips declared on oath that he had not a commission, but was directed by the then Governor to raise a company of Volunteers. Louisa Co., Feb. 14, 1780.

Chapman White, served in Capt. Wm. Phillip's company of Volunteer Rangers in 1763, till legally discharged. Louisa Co., Feb. 14, 1780.

Nathaniel Branham, soldier in Capt. Wm. Phillip's Volunteer company of Rangers in 1763, till legally discharged. Louisa Co., Feb. 14, 1780.

Wm. Brock, soldier in Col. Stephen's Regt. for the defense of the state in 1762, until legally discharged. Orange Co., Dec. 23, 1779.

Wm. Hughes, Sergt. in Capt. Wm. Phillip's volunteer company of Rangers in 1763, till legally discharged. Louisa Co., Feb. 14, 1780.

John Hughes, soldier in Capt. Obediah Woodson's company of Rangers in 1755, till legally discharged, and he is since dead. Proved by oath of Col. Robt. Anderson. Wm. Hughes, heir-at-law. Louisa Co., Feb. 14, 1780.

Wm. Bibb, soldier in Capt. Wm. Phillip's volunteer company of Rangers in 1763, till legally discharged. Louisa Co., Feb. 14, 1780.

James McGehee, soldier in Capt. Wm. Phillip's volunteer company of Rangers in 1763, till legally discharged. Louisa Co., Feb. 14, 1780.

Robt. Hall, soldier in Capt. Wm. Phillip's volunteer company of Rangers in 1763, till legally discharged. Louisa Co., Feb, 14, 1780.

Jeremiah Silf, Sergt. in Capt. McNeal's company of Rangers in 1759, till legally discharged. Louisa Co., Feb. 14, 1780.

Henry Austin, Jnr., and Benj. Austin served in Va. Regt. commanded by Col. Geo. Washington. Sd. Henry as Sergt. and sd. Benj. as Corpl. until their death. Jno. Wilson Austin, heir-at-law to sd. Henry and Benj. King William Co., Feb. 16, 1780.

Jacob Cleet, soldier under command of Col. Byrd in 2d Va. Regt. in 1760. Rockbridge Co., Dec. 7, 1779.

Richd. Sansome, Corpl. in Capt. James Gunn's Co. 1st Va. Regt, in the last war between Great Britain and France. Served to the end of the war. Charlotte Co., Feb. 7, 1780.

Butler Buckley, private in Capt. Thos. Fleming's Co. 1st Va. Regt. in last war between Great Britain and France. Served to end of war. Charlotte Co., Feb. 7, 1780.

James Loggins, Corpl. in Maj. Peachey's Co. 1st Va. Regt. in last war between Great Britain and France. Served to end of war. Charlotte Co., Feb. 7, 1780.

Jno. Monday, decd., and James Russell, served as soldiers in 1760 in a regt. raised for immediate defense of this state. Caroline Co., Feb., 1780.

Henry Cissel and James Cissel, decd., soldiers in 1755 in a regt. raised for immediate defense of the state till properly discharged. Caroline Co., Feb., 1780.

Wm. Cissel, soldier, till properly discharged in 1755 in a regt. raised for immediate defense of the state. Caroline Co., Feb., 1780.

Wm. Mitchell, soldier in a regt. raised for immediate defense of the state in 1758. Caroline Co., Feb., 1780.

Gabriel Throckmorton, entitled to 3,000 acres as Captain the Va. Regt. agreeable to the King's Proc. of 1763. Feb. 24. 1770. Dunmore.

Joseph Parish, Sergt. in 1758 in 2d Va. Regt. raised for immediate defense of the state. Spotsylvania Co., Feb. 17, 1780.

Danl. Simpson, Corpl. in 1758 in 1st Va. Regt. till properly discharged. Spotsylvania Co., Feb. 17, 1780.

James Cooper, soldier in Col. Byrd's Regt. in 1758. Louisa Co., Feb. 14, 1780.

Jno. Dalton, soldier in Capt. Hubbard's Co. of Rangers in 1759. Louisa Co., Feb. 14, 1780.

Jas. Satterwhite, soldier in 1758 in a regt. raised for the immediate defense of the state. Caroline Co. Court, Feb. 1780.

Francis Irvin, soldier in 1755 in a regt. raised for immediate defense of the state. Spotsylvania Co., Feb. 17, 1780.

Wm. Lampton, soldier in 1760 in regt. raised for immediate defense, etc. Spotsylvania Co., Feb. 17, 1780.

Lodowick O'Neal, soldier in 1758 in regt. raised for immediate defense, etc. Spotsylvania Co., 17th day, 1780.

James Ratcliff, soldier in Capt. Wm. Phillip's Vol. Co. of Rangers in 1763 till legally discharged. Louisa Co., Feb. 14, 1780.

James Smith, soldier in Capt. Wm. Phillip's Vol. Co. of Rangers in 1763. Wm. Smith heir-at-law of said James Smith. Louisa Co., Feb. 14, 1780.

Timothy Longest, soldier in 2d Va. Regt., Col. Wm. Byrd commanding; served till regt. was disbanded. Essex Co., Feb. 21, 1780.

Wm. Rogers, soldier in Col. Byrd's Regt. in 1758. Orange Co., Nov. 25, 1779.

James Twopence, soldier in Capt. Wm. Phillip's Vol. Co. of Rangers in 1763, till legally discharged. Louisa Co., Feb. 14, 1780.

Thos. Smith, soldier in 1758 and 1760 in a regt. raised for immediate defense, etc. Caroline Co., Feb. 10, 1780.

Richard Bullard, soldier in Col. Byrd's Regt. in 1758. Orange Co. Nov. 25, 1779.

Thos. Hidgcocks, soldier, till properly discharged, in 1756 in regt. raised for immediate defense, etc. Caroline Co., Feb., 1780.

Wm. Barefoot, soldier in 1st Va. Regt. commanded by Col. Geo. Washington, and continued in service till properly discharged. Essex Co., Feb. 21, 1780.

Richd. Riddle, soldier in 1758 in a regt. raised for immediate defense, etc. Caroline Co. Court, Feb., 1780.

Jno. Jones, drummer in Capt. S. Meredith's Co., Col. Wm. Byrd's Regt., and is entitled to 200 acres of land, under Regal Proc. of 1763. Mar. 26, 1774. (Signed) S. Meredith. Jno. Jones proves services as above in Hanover Co., Feb. 3, 1780.

Joseph Bledsoe, Sergt, in 1st Va. Regt., Col. George Washington commanding, and continued in same till regt. was disbanded. Spotsylvania Co., Feb. 17, 1780.

Daley Longest, soldier in 2d Va. Regt. commanded by Col. Geo. Washington ; continued in same till disbanded. Essex Co., Feb. 21, 1780.

James Gaines, soldier in Col. Byrd's Regt. in 1760. Orange Co., Jan. 27, 1780.

Wm. Gibson, soldier in 1st Va. Regt., commanded by Wm. Byrd, Esq., until same was disbanded. Hanover Co., Feb. 3, 1780.

Jno. Sampson, soldier, till properly discharged, in 1758 in regt. raised for immediate defense, etc. Caroline Co. Court, Feb., 1780.

Benja. Rennold, soldier in 1st Va. Regt. commanded by Col. George Washington. Caroline Co., Feb. 10, 1780.

James Gimber, soldier in 1st Va. Regt. commanded by Col. Geo. Washington, and continued in same till disbanded. Spotsylvania Co., Feb. 14, 1780.

James Tinder, soldier in Col. Byrd's Regt. in 1758. Served his enlistment. Louisa Co., Feb. 14th, 1780.

Jno. Connor, soldier in 1762 in a regt. raised for immediate defense, etc. Spotsylvania Co., Feb. 17, 1880.

James Ratliff, soldier in Capt. Spotswood's Co. of Regulars in 1757, and continued till legally discharged. Louisa Co., Feb. 14, 1780.

Richard Longest, soldier in 2d Va. Regt., commanded by Col. Wm. Byrd, in 1758; continued in same till regt. was disbanded. Essex Co., Feb. 21, 1780.

Richd. Branham, Sergt., till properly discharged, in 1758 in 1st Va. Regt. Spotsylvania Co., Feb. 17, 1780.

Chas. Clark, soldier in 2d Va. Regt., commanded by Col. Wm. Byrd, in 1758, and continued till regt. disbanded. Essex Co., Feb. 21, 1780.

Wm. Camp, Corpl. in 1st Va. Regt., commanded by Col. Geo. Washington, and continued in same till regt. was disbanded. Hanover Co., Feb. 3, 1780.

Wm. Smith, soldier in 1st Va. Regt., commanded by Col. Geo. Washington, and continued till disbanded. Caroline Co., Feb. 10, 1780.

Geo. White (who is since dead), soldier, till properly discharged, in 1758 in a regt. raised for immediate defense, etc. Mary White, widow. Caroline Co., Feb., 1780.

James Arnold, soldier, until properly discharged, in regt. raised for immediate defense in year 1759. Caroline Co., Feb. 21, 1780.

Wm. Robinson (since dead), Sergt., till properly discharged, in 1758 in a regt. raised for immediate defense, etc.   John Robinson, heir-at-law.   Caroline Co. Court, March, 1780.

Joseph Adkins, soldier 1st Va. Regt., commanded by Col. Wm. Byrd, and continued till regt. was disbanded.   Essex Co., Feb. 21, 1780.

Jno. Bullard, soldier in 1st Va. Regt., commanded by Col. Geo. Washington, and continued in same till regt. was disbanded.   Essex Co., Feb. 21, 1780.

Robt. Sanders, Corpl., till properly discharged, in 1760 in a regt. raised for immediate defense, etc.   Spotsylvania Co., Feb. 17, 1780.

Wm. Heath, soldier in corps raised for the defense of Virginia, and commanded by Col. Wm. Byrd, above 20 years ago, and served in same till discharged.   Essex Co., Feb. 21, 1780.

Saml. White, Jr., Corpl. 2d Va. Regt., Col. Wm. Byrd, commanding; continued in said service till his death.   Certf. from Saml. Meredith.   Elias White heir-at-law.   King William Co., Feb. 4, 1780.

Wm. Ross, soldier in 1760, till properly discharged in 1760, in 1st Va. Regt. raised for immediate defense of the state.   Spotsylvania Co., Feb. 11, 1780.

Wm. King, soldier in 1st Va. Regt., commanded by Col. Geo. Washington, and continued in same till disbanded.   Hanover Co., Feb. 3, 1780.

Jno. McCoy, soldier in Capt. Wm. Phillip's Vol. Co. of Rangers in 1763, and continued in same till legally discharged.   Louisa Co., Feb. 14, 1780.

John Sanders, soldier in Capt. Wm. Phillip's Vol. Co. of Rangers in 1763 till legally discharged.   Louisa Co., Feb. 14, 1780.

Rich. Reynolds, soldier, till properly discharged, in the year 1760 in a regt. raised for the immediate defense of the colony.   Spotsylvania Co., Feb. 17, 1780.

Michael Rice, served out enlistment as a non-commissioned officer in Col. Byrd's Regt. in 1758.   Orange Co., Nov. 25, 1779.

Clabourn Routhwell, soldier in Capt. Wm. Phillip's Co. of Vol. Rangers in 1763, till legally discharged.   Louisa Co., Feb. 14, 1780.

Richd. Halbert, soldier, till properly discharged, in a regt. raised for immediate defense of this state.   Spotsylvania Co., Feb. 17, 1780.

Thos. Jones, soldier in Capt. Saml. Overton's Co. of Rangers in 1755 till legally discharged; and also a soldier in Capt. Flemming's Co. of Regulars in 1758 till legally discharged; and also a soldier in Capt. Jno. Posey's Co. of Regulars in 1760 till legally discharged.   Louisa Co., Feb. 14, 1780.

Wm. Turner, soldier, till properly discharged, in year 1760 in a regt. raised for immediate defense, etc.   Spotsylvania Co., Feb. 17, 1780.

Benj. Turner, soldier, till properly discharged, in the year 1758 in a regt. raised for immediate defense of this state.   Spotsylvania Co., Feb. 17, 1780.

Morris Roberts, soldier in Capt. Jno. Fox's Co. of Rangers in 1756, till legally discharged.   Louisa Co., Feb. 14, 1780.

Wm. Fillds (Fields?), soldier, till properly discharged, in 1758 in a regt raised for the defense of this state.   Caroline Co. Court, Feb., 1780.

Chas. Knight, Sergt., till properly discharged, in 1758 in a regt. for immediate defense, etc. Spotsylvania Co., Feb. 17, 1780.

James Samuel, soldier, till properly discharged, in 1754 in regt. raised for immediate defense, etc. Caroline Co. Court, Feb. 1780.

Saml. and George Robinson, served in a corps raised for the defense of Virginia, above 20 years ago, and commanded by Col. Geo. Washington; said Samuel as Sergt. and said George as a soldier, in the same till disbanded. Wm. Robinson, heir-at-law to his two brothers. Essex Co., Feb. 21, 1780.

John Payne, Lieut. in Frontier Batt., last war, under command of Col. Byrd. Williamsburg, March, 1774. Dunmore.

John Hickman, Lieut. in Va. Batt. of Regulars, commanded by Wm. Peachey, Esq., in 1759, and remained till said Batt. was discharged. Hanover Co., Feb. 3, 1780.

James Twopence, soldier in Capt. Christian's Co. of Rangers in 1760, till legally discharged, Louisa Co., Feb. 14, 1780.

David Thompson, Sergt. in Col. Bouquet's Regt. in 1764.

Thos. Dickinson, soldier, till properly discharged, in 1758 in regt. raised for immediate defense of this state. Caroline Co. Court, Feb., 1780.

John Lemay, soldier in Capt. Wm. Phillip's Co. of Vol. Rangers in 1763, till legally discharged. Louisa Co., Feb. 14, 1780.

Francis Self, soldier, till properly discharged, in 1754 in a regt. raised for the defense of this state. Caroline Co., Feb., 1780.

James Floyd, Sergt. in 2d Va. Regt. of Regulars, commanded by Col. Wm. Byrd, in 1758, and served till same was disbanded. King and Queen Co., Feb. 14, 1780.

Benj. Isebell, soldier in Va. Batt. of Regulars, commanded by Wm. Peachey, Esq., in 1759, until disbanded. King and Queen Co., Feb. 14, 1780.

Benj. Clements, served in last war between Great Britain and France as a private in Capt. Wm. Temple's Co. of 1st Va. Regt., and served till end of the war. Charlotte Co., Feb., 1780.

Francis Roberts, private in Capt. Jno. McNeal's Co. 1st Va. Regt. in last war between Great Britain and France, and served to end thereof. Charlotte Co., Feb. 7, 1780.

Jno. Adams, private in Capt. Thos. Woodford's Co. 1st Va. Regt. in last war between Great Britain and France. Charlotte Co., Feb. 7, 1780.

John Perrin, Sergt. in Capt. Jno. McNeal's 1st Va. Regt. in last war between Great Britain and France. Charlotte Co., Feb. 7, 1780.

Richd. Martin, private in Capt. Mordecai Buckner's Co. 1st Va. Regt., in last war between Great Britain and France. Charlotte Co., Feb. 7, 1780.

Isam Crow, Sergt. in 2d Va. Regt. of Regulars, commanded by Col. Wm. Byrd, in 1758, until disbanded. Middlesex Co., Feb. 28, 1780.

Reuben Vass, Lieut. in a Regt. of Regulars, commanded by Wm. Byrd, Esq., in the late war between Great Britain and France.

Thomas Farah, soldier in the Va. Regt. commanded by Adam Stephen, until disbanded. King William Co., Feb. 16, 1780.

Benj. Wheeler, soldier in 2d Va. Regt. of Regulars, commanded by Col. Wm. Byrd, in the year 1758, until disbanded. King and Queen Co., Feb. 11, 1780.

Wm. Phillips, soldier in 2d Va. Regt. of Regulars, commanded by Col. Wm. Byrd in 1760. King and Queen Co., Feb. 14, 1790.

Wm. Jones, soldier in Batt. of Regulars, commanded by Col. Wm. Peachey, in 1759, and continued in same till disbanded. King and Queen Co., Feb. 14, 1780.

James Walden, soldier in 2d Va. Regt. of Regulars, commanded by Col. Wm. Byrd, in 1760, and continued in same till disbanded. King and Queen Co., Feb. 14, 1780.

Geo. Coleman, soldier in 2d Va. Regt. of Regulars, commanded by Col. Wm. Byrd, in 1760, and continued in same till disbanded. King and Queen Co., Feb. 14, 1780.

Henry Finch, entitled to 200 acres of land agreeable to the King's Proc. of 1763. Williamsburg, April 22, 1774. Dunmore.

James Gunn, 3,000 acres of land agreeable to his Majesty's Proc. of 1763. Williamsburg, Dec. 17, 1773. Dunmore.

Chas. Jenkins, soldier in Capt. Saml. Overton's Co. of Rangers in 1755, till legally discharged. Louisa Co., Feb. 14, 1780.

Miles Kenty or Canty, soldier in Capt. Thos. Fleming's Co. of Regulars, in 1758, until legally discharged ; also Sergt. in Capt. John Posey's Co. of Regulars, in 1760. Said Miles being since dead and Anthony Kenty, heir-at-law. Louisa Co., Feb. 14, 1780.

Honble. Wm. Byrd, Esq., entitled, as Col. of the Va. Regt., to 5,000 acres of land agreeable to the King's Proc. of 1763. Williamsburg, Nov. 5, 1773. Dunmore.

John Lamb, soldier in Col. Byrd's Regt. in 1758. Orange Co., Feb. 24, 1780.

Richd. Lamb, soldier in Col. Byrd's Regt. in 1758. Orange Co., Feb. 24, 1780.

Wm. Cave, soldier in Col. Byrd's Regt. in 1759. Orange Co., Feb. 24, 1780.

Wm. Hall, private, and Chas. Travis, drummer, served in King's service for the defense of this state till properly discharged. Richmond Court, Feb., 1780.

Griffing Johnson, served in a corps for the defense of Va., and commanded by Col. Wm. Byrd, and was properly discharged in 1758; and he again served in a corps raised for the same purpose, and commanded by said Byrd, in 1760, and continued in same as a soldier until said regiment was disbanded. Essex Co., Feb. 21, 1780.

Richd. Fouracres, soldier in 1st Va. Regt., commanded by Col. Geo.

LAND BOUNTY CERTIFICATES 27

Washington, and continued in same till disbanded. Spotsylvania Co., Feb. 17, 1780.

Richard Matthews, soldier in Capt. Christopher Hudson's Co. of Regulars, in 1758, till legally discharged; and also corporal in Capt. Meredith's Co. of Regulars, in 1760, until legally discharged. Louisa Co., Feb. 14, 1780.

Wm. Smither, Sr., soldier, till properly discharged, in 1760 in a regt. raised for the immediate defense of the state. Caroline Co., Feb. 10, 1780.

George Turner, soldier in 1st Va. Regt., commanded by Col. Geo. Washington, and continued in same till regt. was disbanded. Caroline Co., Feb. 10, 1780.

Larkin Chew, Ensign 2d Va. Regt., raised in 1758, under command of Col. Byrd, and continued therein till said regt. was disbanded; also Lieut. in 1st Va. Regt., at that time under command of Col. Byrd, and remained therein till said regt. was disbanded; afterwards said Chew entered the regt. commanded by Col. Adam Stephen, and served therein as Lieut. till said regt. was disbanded. Spotsylvania Co., Feb. 17, 1780.

Wm. Daingerfield, Capt. 1st Va. Regt. in 1758, under command of Col. Washington, and continued therein till it was disbanded; and afterwards in a regt. commanded by Adam Stephen in the same capacity of Capt. Spotsylvania Co., Feb. 17, 1780.

Christopher Gist, decd., Captain of Rangers in 1756 for the defense of the frontiers, and served until said company was discharged in 175- (7?). Nathaniel Gist, heir-at-law.

Nathl. Gist, Lieut. in Capt. Christopher Gist's Co. of Rangers in 1756, and served till the company was reduced in 1757; and also as a Capt. in Col. Geo. Washington's regt., called the 1st Va. Regt., raised in 1756 and disbanded in 1762, and that he continued in the regt. until disbanded; also as a Capt. in the regt. commanded by Col. Adam Stephen, raised in 1762, and continued as Capt. until that was disbanded. Spotsylvania Co., Feb. 17, 1780.

Jno. Bradford, Corp. in 2d Va. Regt., commanded by Col. Wm. Byrd. Certificate from Capt. Saml. Meredith. King William Co., Feb. 16, 1780.

Jno. Brown, soldier in 2d Va. Regt. of Regulars, commanded by Col. Wm. Byrd, in 1758, till same was disbanded. King and Queen Co., Feb. 14, 1780.

Thos. Davis, Sergt. in 2d Va. Regt., Col. Wm. Byrd commanding, in 1756, and continued till disbanded. King and Queen Co., Feb. 14, 1780.

Chas. Turner, soldier in 2d Va. Regt. of Regulars, Col. Wm. Byrd commanding, in 1758, till disbanded. King and Queen Co., Feb. 14, 1780.

Wm. Barlow, soldier in 2d Va. Regt. of Regulars, Col. Wm. Byrd commanding, in 1758, till disbanded. King and Queen Co., Feb. 14, 1780.

Jno. Harvey, soldier in 2d Va. Regt. of Regulars, Col. Wm. Byrd commanding, in 1758, till disbanded. King and Queen Co., Feb. 14, 1780.

Thomas and William Cooper, both of whom served in the Va. Regt. commanded by Col. Wm. Byrd in the war between Great Britain and France, upwards of 20 years ago, till same was disbanded. James Cooper, heir-at-law to his two brothers. Essex Co., Feb. 25, 1780.

John O'Neal, soldier in Va. Regt. commanded by Col. Wm. Peachey, till regiment was disbanded.   Certificate signed by Jno. Hickman, Gent.   King William Co., Feb., 1780.

Edmond Foster, soldier in Capt. Saml. Overton's Co. of Rangers in 1756 until legally discharged. By cert. under hand of Capt. Saml. Meredith, it appears that said Foster was soldier in Col. Byrd's regiment in 1758. Louisa Co., Feb. 14, 1780.

Wm. Wousley (Moseley?), soldier in Capt. Gunn's Co. of Regulars in 1758, till legally discharged, also soldier in Capt. Meredith's Co. of Rangers in 1759, till legally discharged. Louisa Co., Feb. 14, 1780.

David Stewart, deceased, principal commissary on Col. Andrew Lewis' Expedition against the Indians in 1758.   John Stewart, son and heir.   Greenbrier Co., Feb., 1780.

Geo. Underwood, entitled to 200 acres of land for services in last war agreeable to Proc. of 1763. Williamsburg, April 16, 1774. Dunmore.

Matthew Roberts, a free negro, who served as a soldier in 1st Va. Regt., is entitled to 50 acres of land by His Majesty's Proc. of 1763. Dec. 16, 1773. Dunmore.

Wm. Foster, soldier in Capt. Saml. Overton's Co. of Rangers in 1755, till legally discharged. Said Foster also was a soldier in said Overton's Co. of Rangers in 1756, till legally discharged. Louisa Co., Feb. 14, 1780.

Thomas Mourning, soldier in Va. Batt. under command Wm. Byrd, Esq., in 1758, till legally discharged. Hanover Co., Mar. 2, 1780.

Benj. Oliver, soldier till properly discharged in 1758, in a regiment raised for immediate defense, etc. Caroline Co., Feb. 10, 1780.

Eustace Howard, soldier in 2nd Va. Reg. of Regulars, commanded by Col. Wm. Byrd in 1758, till legally discharged. Middlesex Co., Feb. 28, 1780.

Jno. McKendree, Sergt. 2nd Va. Regt. of Regulars, commanded by Col. Wm. Byrd, till legally discharged. King and Queen Co., Feb. 14, 1780.

Wm. Halliard, soldier in 2nd Va. Regt. of Regulars, commanded by Col. Wm. Byrd in 1758, till legally discharged. King and Queen Co., Feb. 14, 1780.

Wm. Byrd, Col. 2nd Va. Regt. of Regulars till same was disbanded in 1758; also Col. in the Va. Regt. in 1759, 1760, 1761 and part of 1762. Certf. from the Hustings Court of Williamsburg. February 9, 1780. Presented by Mary Byrd, Executrix of the last will and testament of the Honble. Wm. Byrd, deceased.

Jno. Smith, deceased, Lieut. in Capt. Jno. Smith's Co. of Rangers, 1756, raised in this state, and was killed at Fort Vause when attacked by the enemy, French and Indians, in that year. Abraham Smith, brother and heir-at-law of John Smith, deceased. Rockingham Co., Nov. 23, 1779.

Thos. Standley, Corpl. in 2nd Va. Regt. commanded by Wm. Byrd, till same was disbanded. Certf. from Saml. Meredith, Gent.

Stephen Smith, soldier in 2nd Va. Regt. commanded by Wm. Byrd, till same was disbanded. King William Co., Feb. 16, 1780.

Benj. Harris, deceased, soldier in Capt. Christopher Hudson's Co. of Rangers in 1758, until legally discharged. Fredk. Harris, guardian to Overton Harris, heir-at-law to said Benj. Harris. Louisa Co., Feb. 14, 1780.

Chas. Barrett, Sergt. in Capt. Wm. Phillip's Co. of Vol. Rangers in 1763, until legally discharged. Louisa Co., Feb. 14, 1780.

Robt. Goodwin, soldier in Capt. Wm. Phillip's Vol. Company of Rangers in 1763, until legally discharged. Louisa Co., Feb. 14, 1780.

James Bullock, Ensign in Capt. Wm. Phillip's Co. of Vol. soldiers in 1763, until said company was discharged. Hanover Co., Mar. 2, 1780.

Philip Cosby, soldier in Capt. Wm. Phillip's Co. of Vol. Rangers in 1763. Said Cosby is since dead and David Cosby is heir-at-law. Louisa Co., Feb. 14, 1780.

James Ward, deceased, Lieut. in Capt. McClannehan's Co. under command of Col. Bouquet on an expedition against the Indians in 1764. Wm. Ward, son and heir of said deceased. Williamsburg, Mar. 6, 1780.

Solomon Carpenter, deceased, soldier in Capt. Dickerson's Co of Rangers for protection and defense of the frontiers of Va. in 1758-59. Thos. Carpenter heir-at-law. Botetourt Court, Feb., 1780.

Ezekiel Johnson, soldier in Capt. Dickerson's Co. of Rangers on frontiers of the Colony, 1757-58 and 1759. Botetourt Co., Feb., 1780.

Richard Evans, soldier 1763 in war between Great Britain and France, until properly discharged. Essex Co., Feb. 21, 1780.

Augustine Ramsey, soldier in war between Great Britain and France, upwards of 20 years ago, until properly discharged. Essex Co., Feb. 21, 1780.

John Sallard (Tallard?), of Richmond Co., subaltern officer in 1759, 1760 and 1761 in regiments commanded by Col. Wm. Byrd and others, until properly discharged. Richmond Co., Mar. 6, 1780.

John Horn, decd., non-commissioned officer under Col. Mercer in the late war in 1758, in which service said Horn died. John Avis, legal representative. Culpeper Co., Feb. 21, 1780.

Colby Chew, Lieut. in Va. Regt. in 1758 under Col. Washington, and was wounded by the Indians by which he was drowned in the waters of the Ohio. Benj. Johnston, in behalf of Joseph Chew, legal representative of Colby Chew.

Mordecai Buckner, Capt. in Col. Adam Stephen's Regt. raised in 1758 by this state, till properly discharged. Culpeper Co., Feb. 21, 1780.

Neil McCauley, soldier in 1758 in Capt. John Field's company in Col. Wm. Byrd's regiment, till properly discharged. Culpeper Co., Feb. 21, 1780.

James Black, soldier in 1758 under Gen. Braddock, and served until discharged. Culpeper Co., Feb. 21, 1780.

Edward Jones, Corpl., and Wm. Jones, soldier, under Col. Geo. Washington in 1758, both of whom died in the service of this state. Culpeper Co., Feb. 21, 1780.

John Summers, Sergt. in 2nd Va. Regt. under command of Col. Wm. Byrd. Williamsburg, May 7, 1774. Dunmore.

Chas. Scott, Esq., private, Corpl., Sergt., Ensign 1st Va. Regt. raised in Va. before the Proclamation of the King in 1763. General Court held in Town of Richmond, Mar. 2, 1780.

Edwd. Foley, soldier in 1760, 1st Va. Regt. raised for immediate defense, etc., until properly discharged. Spotsylvania Co., Feb. 17, 1780.

Benjamin Temple, Lieut. in Va. Batt. of Regulars, commanded by Col. Wm. Peachey in 1759, until properly discharged. Hanover Co., Mar. 2, 1780.

Holt Richeson, Lieut. in Va. Batt. of Regulars, commanded by Wm. Peachey, Esqr., in 1759, until properly discharged. Hanover Co., Mar. 2, 1780.

James Riddle, non-commissioned officer in Capt. Hogg's Co. of Rangers in 1758. Orange Co., Feb. 24, 1780.

Anthony Hughes, soldier in Capt. Stubb's Co., under command of Col. Byrd, in French war in 1760, until legally discharged. Fluvanna Co., Feb. 3, 1780.

Capt. John Smith, entitled as Capt. of the new levies, to 3,000 acres agreeable to King's Proc. of 1763. Dec. 16, 1773. Dunmore.

James May, soldier in Col. Washington's Regt. from 1756-1762 till properly discharged. Frederick Co., Mar. 9, 1780.

David Kennedy, quarter-master to a troop of light horse in the service of the Colony of Va., commanded by Capt. Robert Stewart, and served therein until troop was reduced. Appointed in year 1755. In year 1756 was appointed Deputy Commissary under Dr. Thos. Walker to the troops serving on the Va. frontiers, and served about 2 years. In 1758 was appointed Quarter-master to the Va. regiment commanded by Col. Washington, and likewise appointed Ensign in the said regiment in which capacities he served until the regiment was reduced. When a regiment was raised in 1762, under command of Col. Adam Stephen, he was appointed Lieut., under which commission he likewise acted as Quarter-master until the regiment was reduced. Frederick Co. Court, Feb., 1780.

Reuben Vass, Lieut. until properly discharged, in the campaign of 1758, also campaign of 1762, in different regiments raised for the defense of this state. Caroline Co. Court, Mar., 1780.

Thos. Hutcherson, soldier till properly discharged in the campaign of 1760 in different regiments raised for the defense of the state. Caroline Co., Mar., 1780.

Jno. Johnson, soldier in 1758 in a regiment raised for the immediate defense of the state, till properly discharged. Caroline Co. ——

James Taylor, Ensign in Capt. Hogg's Co. of Rangers in 1758. Caroline Co., Mar. 9, 1780.

Richd. Johnston, Gent., Lieut. in the campaigns of 1758, also in the campaign of 1759, in different regiments raised for immediate defense of this state.

Thos. Morris, soldier till properly discharged in 1759 in a regiment for the immediate defense of this state. Orange Co., Feby., 1780.

Freeman Lewelling, John Gaulding, Chas. Howall and James Foster, severally privates in late war between Great Britain and France, under command of Col. Wm. Byrd, and continued in service during their enlistments. Prince Edward Co., Feby. Court, 1780.

Edwd. Penix, deceased, soldier under command of the late Hon. Wm. Byrd, Esqr., until he was discharged, and on his return the said Penix died. Jeremiah Penix, heir-at-law. Prince Edward Co., Feby. Court, 1780.

Nathan Gibson, soldier in Capt. Christian's Co. of Rangers in 1760 till legally discharged. Louisa Co., Nov. 18, 1779.

James Melton, soldier in Capt. Overton's Co. of Rangers in 1756 till legally discharged; also soldier in Capt. Posey's Co. in year 1758 till legally discharged. Louisa Co., Oct. 11, 1779.

Wm. Melton, soldier in Capt. Christian's Co. of Rangers; soldier in Capt. Overton's Co. of Rangers in 1756; soldier in Capt. Hudson's Co. in 1758, till legally discharged. Louisa Co., Oct. 11, 1779.

Ansolem Clarkson, soldier in Capt. Overton's Co. of Rangers in 1755 till legally discharged; served twice as a Sergeant in said company in 1756 till properly discharged. Louisa Co., Oct. 11, 1779.

Wm. Ahorn, soldier in Capt. Overton's Co. of Rangers in 1756 till discharged. Louisa Co., Nov. 8, 1779.

Anthony Thompson, soldier in Capt. Jos. Fox's Co. of Rangers in 1756 till legally discharged. Louisa Co., Feb. 14, 1780.

Dumas Lane, soldier in Capt. Christian's Co. of Rangers in 1760 till legally discharged. Louisa Co., Oct. 11, 1779.

Jno. Shepperson, soldier in Capt. Overton's Co. of Rangers in 1756 till legally discharged. Louisa Co., Oct. 11, 1779.

Thos. Buford, deceased, Sergt. under Gen. Braddock in 1754, and was discharged. Sergt. again under Braddock in 1755. Lieut. under Col. Washington in 1756 ; Lieut. under Col. Byrd in 1758 ; Lieut. in another regiment under Col. Byrd in 1759.

James Buford, Gent., guardian of John Buford and executor of Thos. Buford, deceased, aforesaid. Bedford Co., Feby. Court, 1780.

Joseph Ray, Cadet in the Va. Regt., marched up to Fort Ligeneve where he was appointed by Genl. Stanwix as Supt. of a company of Artificers and received Captain's pay, and continued in same station during the campaign of 1759, and until the army retired to winter quarters. Augusta Co., Nov. 17, 1779.

Miles Kenty, decd., soldier in Capt. Thos. Fleming's Co. of Regulars in 1758 till legally discharged. Anthony Kenty, heir-at-law.

Miles Kenty, deceased, Sergt. in Capt. Jno. Posey's Co. of Regulars in 1760 till legally discharged. Anthony Kenty, heir-at-law. Louisa Co., Feb. 14, 1780.

Gen. Geo. Weedon, Capt.-Lieut. 1st Va. Regt., also served in Col. Adam Stephen's Regt. from time it was raised till it was discharged, with rank of Capt. Spotsylvania Co., Feb. 17, 1780.

Jacob Sharp, entitled to 50 acres of land, agreeable to the King's Proc. of 1763. March 29, 1774. Dunmore.

Thos. Poo, entitled to 50 acres of land, agreeable to the King's Proc. of 1763. May 29, 1774 Dunmore.

Wm. Oglesby, soldier in Col. Byrd's Va. Regt. and thereby entitled to 50 acres of land under Proc. of 1763. Dec. 14, 1773. Dunmore.

Wm. Flanders, soldier in Va. Regt. under command of Col. Wm. Byrd, and is entitled to 50 acres of land under Proc. of 1763. Dec. 14, 1773. Dunmore.

Thos. Craddock, entitled to 200 acres of land as a fifer under King's Proc. of 1763. Williamsburg, June 2, 1774. Dunmore.

Bartlet Ford, entitled to 50 acres of land as a soldier in the late war, agreeable to King's Proclamation of 1763. Williamsburg, June 2, 1774. Dunmore.

Moses Parrish, entitled to 50 acres of land under King's Proc., 1763, as a soldier in last war. Williamsburg, May 17, 1774.

Wm. Blunkall, entitled to 200 acres of land as a Corpl. in the last war agreeable to King's Proc. of 1763. Williamsburg, May 12, 1774. Dunmore.

Stephen Atkins, entitled to 50 acres of land as a soldier in late war, agreeable to King's Proc. of 1763. Williamsburg, June 2, 1774. Dunmore.

Chas. Jordan, entitled to 200 acres of land as a Sergt. in the late war, agreeable to King's Proc. of 1763. Williamsburg, June 2, 1774. Dunmore.

Joseph Stephens, decd., Major and Engineer in 1758 in a Regt. raised for the immediate defense of this state. Richard Stevens, son and heir-at-law of said Jos. Stephens.

Jno. Reeves, decd., soldier in Capt. Blagg's Company, Col. Adam Stephen's Regt. five years, and was discharged by virtue of an Act of Assembly for that purpose. Saml. Howard, son-in-law to said John Reeves. Buckingham Co., Feb. 14, 1780.

Jno. Baker Turner, Christopher Fielding and Patrick Ritchie served as soldiers in the 1st Va. Regt. commanded by Col. Washington. Jos. Grimsley and John Brumley, soldiers in 2nd Va. Regt. commanded by Col. Byrd. Culpeper Co., Feb. 21, 1780.

Wm. Poulter enlisted as a soldier under Alexr. Waugh in 1759, and served in Col. Byrd's Regt., on the frontiers of Va. Culpeper Co., Dec. 20, 1779.

Hancock Eustace, Esqr., entitled to 3,000 acres of land agreeable to the King's Proc. of 1763. Williamsburg, Dec. 30, 1773. Dunmore.

Wm. Peachey, Gent., served as Lieut.-Col. Commanding, of the Frontier Battl. in 1759 till same was properly discharged. Richmond Co., Mar. 6, 1780.

Wm. Peachey, Gent., Capt. in regiment commanded by Col. Geo. Washington in 1755, 1756 and 1757, and continued in same till it was reduced. Richmond Co., March 6, 1780.

Jno. Hughes, soldier in the Va. Regt. and is entitled to 50 acres of land under the King's Proc. of 1763. Williamsburg, April 15, 1774. Dunmore.

Thos. Sanders, soldier in the 2nd Va. Regt. under command of Capt. Jno. Lightfoot in the last French and Indian war. New Kent Co., Mar. 9, 1780.

W. Bowles, soldier in the 2d Va. Regt., Col. Wm. Byrd commanding.

Certf. by Saml. Meredith, Gent., who served as a Capt. in the late war between Great Britain and France. Chas. Tyler, heir-at-law. Henrico Co., Feb., 1780.

James Moss, is entitled to 50 acres of land as a soldier in the late war, agreeable to the King's Proc. of 1763. Williamsburg, April 20, 1774. Dunmore.

James Mercer, Esqr., makes oath that two of his brothers, Geo. Mercer and John Fenton Mercer, were in the service of the State in 1754. Geo. Mercer as Captain and John Fenton Mercer, Ensign, in a Va. Regt. raised for the defense of the frontiers of this state commanded by Col. Joshua Fry, and continued in said service till said regiment was reduced. That in the year 1755 in the expedition against Fort Duquesne the said George commanded an independent company and the said John Fenton was appointed a Lieutenant of Horse, commanded by Capt. Robert Stewart, in which service they continued till that corps was discharged. That in the old Va. Regt. commanded by Col. George Washington, the said George and John Fenton Mercer commanded companies and continued therein till the said John Fenton was killed by the enemy, and the said George was promoted to the rank of Lieut.-Col. in the 2nd Va. Regt. commanded by Hon. Wm. Byrd, until the same was reduced. The said George is heir-at-law to the said John Fenton Mercer. At Genl. Crt. held in Richmond Town, Va., March 22, 1780. James Mercer, Atto. for Geo. Mercer.

Chas. Dick, Esq., commissioned and acted as a commissary of provisions and horses for the Va. troops sometime in the year 1754, and continued therein until army was provided for by contract which superseded his appointment. He was also commissioned and acted in like department for the British troops in this State on the expedition against Ft. Duquesne, and so served until his appointment was superseded by occasion of the army's being supplied by contract. Genl. Crt., Richmond, Va., March 22, 1780.

James Mercer, Esqr., decd., was an inhabitant of this State before 1745 and left same as an officer of a company raised here, on the expedition against Carthagena and returned here in 1755 as a captain in the 18th Regt. of Foot, commanded by Col. Dunbar on an expedition against Fort Duquesne. That he acted in the same regiment till his death, which happened in North America some time in the year 1758 or 1759, when he was a Major. That at the time of his death John Mercer of Stafford Co. became his heir, as his only brother who died in the year 1768, and by his will and under his title John Francis Mercer, an infant, then and still an inhabitant of this State, is entitled to the land under the King's Proc. of 1763. Genl. Crt., Richmond, Va., March 22 1780.

Mordecai Buckner, Gent., Capt. till properly discharged, in a Regt. raised for immediate defense of this state under command of Col. Stephen in 1762. Essex.

Mordecai Buckner, Gent. Quarter-master, till properly discharged, in 1755, in the forces raised for immediate defense of this state, whereof Adam Stephen, Gent., was eldest Capt. Essex.

Wm. Madison, decd., Corpl. in Va. Regt. under my command. Signed. March 31, 1774. W. Byrd. Thos. Arbuthnott, heir, of Essex Co., March 20, 1780.

Jno. Stadler, Lieut. in Penna, Regt. under command of Col. Armstrong, entitled under King's Proc. of 1763. Jan. 8, 1774. Dunmore.

Jno. Johnson, soldier in Capt. Peter Hogg's Co. of Rangers in 1758, till legally discharged. Louisa Co., March 31, 1780.

Col. Zachary Lewis, Lieut. in 1756 till legally discharged, "as recruiting officer enlisted 30 men and passed them at the general rendezvous at Winchester in 1758, but did not get a commission of a Captain although he had an unconditional promise for the same by the late Pres. Blair." Louisa Co., March 13, 1780.

Francis Barnes, soldier in 1758 under Gen. Forbes. Culpeper Co., Jan. 17, 1780.

Thos. Murphy, soldier in 1758 under Gen. Forbes. Culpeper Co., Jan. 17, 1780.

Danl. McCarty, decd., soldier in Va. Regt. under my command, and that Sarah Raines, wife of Giles Raines, is sister and heiress-at-law of said Daniel McCarty. May 6, 1774. W. Byrd. Said McCarty served in 2nd Va. Regt. in Capt. Jno. Roote's Co. New Kent Co., March 2, 1780. Proved by Giles Raines.

Thos. Hutcheson, soldier till properly discharged in 1758 and 1760 in a regiment raised for immediate defense of the state. Caroline Co.

Nathan Holloway, soldier till properly discharged in 1762 in a regiment raised for immediate defense of the state. Caroline Co., March Crt., 1780.

Wm. McCormick, Lieut. in a Co. of Rangers in the Va. service in Col. Henry Bouquet's campaign. Yohogania Co., Feb., 1780.

Isaac Cox, Ensign, in a corps of Rangers raised in Va. and in actual service in Col. Henry Bouquet's campaign in 1763. Yohogania Co., Oct., 1779.

George McCarmick, Ensign in a Co. of Rangers in Va. service in Col. Henry Bouquet's campaign in 1763. Yohogania Co., Feb., 1780.

Jacob Morris, Sergt. in the service of Va. is entitled to 200 acres of land under the King's Proc. of 1763. Feb. 14, 1774. Dunmore.

Samuel Burton, private in the regiment commanded by the late Hon. Wm. Byrd, Esq., in the late war between Gt. Britain and France. Prince Edward Co., March, 1780.

Jonathan Smith, Lieut. in the Regular service in the late war between Gt. Britain and France, in the Regt. commanded by the late Hon. Wm. Byrd, Esq. Prince Edward Co., March, 1780.

Robt. Rayburn, entitled to 100 acres of land agreeable to King's Proc. of 1763. March 29, 1774. Dunmore.

Thos. Hitchcock, soldier in 1763 in a regiment raised for immediate defense of this state, commanded by Col. Wm. Byrd. Essex Co., Feb., 1780.

Newman Boulware, decd., soldier in 1760 in a regiment raised for the immediate defense of this state. Margt., Jennitt and Elizabeth Boulware, co-heirs of said Newman Boulware. Caroline Co., March, 1780.

Wm. Rennolds, soldier till properly discharged in 1758 in a regiment raised for immediate defense, etc. Caroline Co., March Crt., 1780.

Thos. Thorp, Corpl. till properly discharged in 1760 in a regiment raised for immediate defense, etc. Caroline Co., March, 1780.

Saml. Taylor, soldier in 1758 in a regiment raised for immediate defense, etc. Caroline Co., March, 1780.

Jno. Carter, soldier in 1758 in a regiment raised for immediate defense, etc. Caroline Co., March, 1780.

Lemuel Barret, entitled to 3,000 acres of land agreeable to Proc. of 1763. March 30, 1774. Dunmore.

Zaccheus Cosby, soldier in Capt. Wm. Phillip's Co. of Vol. Rangers in 1763, and continued in same till legally discharged. Louisa Co., Feb. 14, 1780.

Wm. Edwards, soldier in Capt. Walter Stewart's Co. of Regulars in 1758, till legally discharged. Louisa Co., March 13, 1780.

James Cowper, enlisted under Richd. Johnson of Caroline as a soldier in 1760 ; served till legally discharged under Capt. Chas. Scott in his Co. of Regulars. Louisa Co., March 13, 1780.

James Garrett, entitled to 200 acres of land as a Sergt. in the late war agreeable to Proc. of 1763. Williamsburg, April 25, 1774. Dunmore.

Jno. Lawson, entitled to 2,000 acres of land under Proc. of 1763. Williamsburg, Dec. 30, 1773. Dunmore.

Robt. Hughes, soldier in Va. Regt. and is entitled to 50 acres of land under Proc. of 1763. Williamsburg, April 15, 1774. Dunmore.

In winter of 1774, Lord Dunmore then governor of Va. granted a warrant for 2,000 acres of land located in Augusta Co., unto Lieut. Alex. McDonnald, which in March, 1774, said McDonnald sold unto Jno. Cary and Jno. Swan. (No date.)

Thos. Price, Esq., Capt. in Penna. Regt. under command of Col. Mercer, is entitled to 3,000 acres agreeable to Proc. of 1763. February 28, 1774. Dunmore.

Wm. Thomson entitled to 3,000 acres of land under Proc. of 1763. Williamsburg, April 2, 1774. Dunmore.

Robert Breckenridge, Gentl., decd., commanded a company of soldiers that was incorporated with a detachment of the 1st Va. Regt. in 1756 ; served in the expedition commanded by Col. Andrew Lewis against the Shawnees that year, till the company was disbanded. Alex. Breckenridge heir-at-law to said Robert. Botetourt Crt., Dec., 1779.

John Heland, enlisted as a soldier in 1756 in the old Va. Regt. and served therein 4 years, and was discharged for infirmities as appears from his discharge from Col. Wm. Byrd, who then commanded the regiment. Frederick Co., March 18, 1780.

James Keeling, Corpl. in the Va. Regt. of regulars, commanded by Col. Washington, raised for the last war and continued therein till sd. regt. was disbanded in 1762. Frederick Co., Mar. 8, 1780.

Adam Stephen, Esqr. in 1754 appointed eldest Captain in corps raised and commanded by Col. Fry ; upon death of Col. Fry he was promoted to rank of Major or Lieut. Col. in said corps and served therein during the period for which the said corps was raised. He was appointed paymaster to the troops raised in winter of 1754 and spring of 1755, and acted as such until superseded by the appointment of Mr. Byrd in April. Under command of Genl. Braddock he acted as Capt. Commandant and eldest officer at that time in Virginia service upon the said Braddock's expedition. When Col. Washington resumed the command of the Va. Regt. he was appointed Lieut. Col. thereof and served in that capacity under said Washington and afterwards under Col. Byrd until the regiment was reduced in spring of 1762. That he commanded the Va. Regt. raised in the year 1762. Frederick Co., Mar. 8, 1780.

Gabriel Throckmorton, appointed in 1758 Lieut. in a regiment commanded by Col. Byrd and served in that capacity until the same was disbanded. In 1759 he was appointed a Capt. in a Battl. raised for the defense of the frontiers, commanded by Col. Wm. Peachey, and served therein till same was disbanded in 1760. Frederick Co., Mar. 8, 1780.

Saml. Sparks, soldier in 1754 in the Battle of the Meadows and afterwards enlisted in the old Va. Regt. commanded by Col. Washington, and continued therein till same was disbanded. Frederick Co., Mar. 9, 1780.

Jno. Creagh, entitled to 200 acres of land as a Sergt. in late war under Proc. of 1763. Williamsburg, May 14, 1774. Dunmore.

Jno. Poasdell, Sergt. in 1st Va. Regt. until same was disbanded. Stafford Co., Feb., 1780.

Richd. Griffin and John Osbourn, both soldiers in Capt. Robt. Mumford's Co.; James Owen, Thos. Chamberlyne and Stephen Mallett, in Capt. Gunn's Co.; and Saml. Bentley in Capt. Saml. Meredith's Co., belonging to Col. Wm. Byrd's regiment, and that they all served to close of the war. Mecklenburg Co., Feb. 14, 1780.

Jno. Farrar, Sergt. in Capt. James Walker's Co., in the last war in Col. Byrd's Regt. and served until legally discharged. Mecklenburg Co., Mar. 13, 1780.

Thos. Matthews, soldier in Capt. James Gunn's Co.; Wm. Watts, soldier in Capt. Jno. Smith's Co.; all belonging to the Regt. commanded by Col. Wm. Byrd; Wm. Avery served as soldier in Capt. Jno. McNeil's Co., 1st Va. Regt. They were all soldiers in last war between Gt. Britain and France, and served to close of the war. Mecklenburg Co., Mar. 13, 1780.

Dabney Carr, decd., soldier in Capt. Wm. Phillip's Co. Vol. Rangers in 1763 till legally discharged. Louisa Co., Feb. 14, 1780.

Michael Reasoner, entitled to 50 acres of land agreeable to Proc. of the King in 1763. Williamsburg, Feb. 14, 1774. Dunmore.

Thos. Lewis entitled to 200 acres of land under Proc. of 1763. May 22, 1774. Dunmore.

John Bridge entitled to 50 acres of land agreeable to Proc. of 1763. May 22, 1774. Dunmore.

Jno. Hall, Sergt. in Capt. Wm. Phillip's Co. of Rangers in 1763 till legally discharged. Sd. Jno. Hall is since dead and Wm. Lipscomb is Guard. to Eliz. and Sarah Hall, co-heirs said John Hall. Louisa Co., Mar. 13, 1780.

Richard Phillips, soldier in Capt. Joseph Fox's Co. of Rangers in 1755, until legally discharged. Louisa Co., Mar. 13, 1780.

Jno. Freeman, soldier in Capt. Wm. Phillip's Co. of Rangers in 1763 till legally discharged. Louisa Co., Mar. 13, 1780.

John Wheelor, soldier in 1758 till his death. Moses Wheelor heir-at-law to sd. John. Louisa Co., Mar. 13, 1780.

Thos. Bibb, 1st Lieut. in Capt. Jos. Fox's Co. of Vol. Rangers in 1755 till legally discharged. Said Bibb is dead and Richard Phillips is his executor. Louisa Co., Mar. 13, 1780.

Wm. Wheelor, soldier in 1758 till his death and Moses Wheelor is his heir-at-law. Louisa Co., Mar. 13, 1780.

By the oath of Capt. Joseph Fox it appears that Capt. William Phillips enlisted and served in his Co. of Rangers in the year 1755 till legally discharged. Louisa Co., Mar. 13, 1780.

Joseph Hopkins, Jnr., Sergt. in Capt. James Gunn's Co. of Regulars in 1759 till legally discharged. Louisa Co., Mar. 13, 1780.

Chas. Hester, soldier in Capt. Wm. Phillip's Co. of Vol. Rangers in 1763 till legally discharged. Louisa Co., Feb. 14, 1780.

Capt. Wm. Hughes enlisted and served part of his time as a Sergt. in Capt. Wm. Phillip's Co. of Vol. Rangers in 1763 ; one of Capt. Phillip's Lieuts. being killed, the said Hughes did duty as Ensign till legally discharged, receiving pay of an Ensign. Louisa Co., Mar. 13, 1780.

John Hill entitled to 200 acres of land as Sergt. in the late war agreeable to the King's Proc. of 1763. Williamsburg, May 17, 1774. Dunmore.

John Clark served as Sergt. in 1st Va. Regt. and is entitled to 200 acres of land agreeable to the King's Proc. of 1763. Williamsburg, May 22, 1774. Dunmore.

John Dickinson Littlepage, entitled to 2,000 acres of land "for his servis as ensign in ye Va. servis," agreeable to King's Proc. of 1763. Jan. 31, 1774. Dunmore.

Daniel Tilman, Sergt. in Capt. Flemming's Co. under command of Wm. Peachey, Col. of the Frontier Battl. in 1758 ; until legally discharged. Fluvanna Co., Apr. 6, 1780.

George Ehrmantrout, soldier in Capt. Hogg's Co. of Rangers and continued in the service until discharged in 1758. Rockingham Co., Apr. 24, 1780.

Danl. Grubb, soldier in Capt. Hogg's Co. of Rangers, and continued in the service until the said company was discharged in 1758. Rockingham Co., Apr. 24, 1780.

Abraham Moone, soldier in Capt. Bullett's Co. of Regulars in last war, till legally discharged. Botetourt Co., March, 1780.

John Hooker, soldier in old Va. Regt. commanded by Col. Geo. Washington (enlisted when same was raised), also appointed non-commissioned officer in said company in which capacity he served until it was disbanded. Frederick Co., Apr. 4, 1780.

Stephen Blankenship, soldier in 1st Va. Regt. of Regulars, raised during the late war between Gt. Britain and France and continued in said Regt.

until he was taken prisoner by the enemy, with whom he continued till the end of the war. Genl. Crt. held in town of Richmond, Mar. 2, 1780.

Wm. Jenkins, soldier in the old Va. Regt. in late war, wherein he served during the whole war. Frederick Co., May 2, 1780.

Wm. Banton enlisted in 1760 in Col. Byrd's Regt. of Regulars raised during the late war between Gt. Britain and France till legally discharged. Chesterfield Co., Apr. 7, 1780.

Smith Williamson, soldier in regular service in Col. Byrd's Regt. entitled to 50 acres of land. Rockbridge Co., Sept., 1779.

David Graham, deceased, soldier in Capt. Wm. Preston's Co. of Rangers in late war between Gt. Britain and France in 1758. John Graham guardian to Joseph Graham. Augusta Co., Mar. 21, 1780.

Jeremiah Blewford, soldier in regiment commanded by Col. William Byrd in the last Indian war in America. King George Co., Apr. Court, 1780.

Linn Banks, soldier in 1759; Sergt. in 1760 in Va. troops under command of Col. Wm. Byrd in late war. Amherst Co., Feb., 1780.

John Wiley, soldier in the regular additional troops to the Va. Regt. during the Cherokee expedition in 1760, commanded by Col. Byrd; about six months, till legally discharged. Montgomery Co., May, 1780.

John Dastforan, decd., soldier in 1758 and 1759 in a company of Rangers under Robert Rutherford's command, until same was reduced. Berkeley, Court, March, 1780.

Edward Luce, Sergt. in Capt. Robert. Rutherford's Co. of Rangers until same was reduced. Berkeley, Mar., 1780.

Jonathan Seaman, Corpl. in 1758 and 1759 in a company of Rangers under command of Capt. Robert Rutherford, till same was reduced. Berkeley Co., March, 1780.

Thos. Bright, soldier in 1758, in Capt. Robert Rutherford's Co. of Rangers till same was reduced. Berkeley Co., Mar., 1780.

Alex. Lemon, soldier in 1758 and 1759, in Capt. Robert Rutherford's Co. of Rangers till same was reduced. Berkeley Co., March, 1780.

Joseph Hedge, soldier in 1758 and 1759 in Capt. Robt. Rutherford's Co. of Rangers till it was reduced. Berkeley Co., March, 1780.

James Shirley, soldier in 1758 and 1759, in Capt. Robt. Rutherford's Co. of Rangers till it was reduced. Berkeley Co., Mar. Crt., 1780.

Jacob Rush, soldier in 1758 and 1759, in Capt. Rutherford's Co. of Rangers until it was reduced. Berkeley Co., Mar., 1780.

Walter Shirley, soldier in 1758 and 1759, in Capt. Robt. Rutherford's Co. of Rangers, till same was reduced. Berkeley Co., Mar., 1780.

John Rouse, Sergt. in 1758 and 1759, in Capt. Robt. Rutherford's Co. of Rangers, until same was reduced. Berkeley Co., Mar., 1780.

Richard Bowen, soldier in 1758 and 1759 in Capt. Robt. Rutherford's Co. of Rangers, until it was reduced. Berkeley Co., Mar., 1780.

Thos. Edmondson, entitled to 200 acres of land under Proc. of 1763. Williamsburg, Apr. 18, 1774. Dunmore.

Wm. Easley, soldier in last French and Indian war, eight months under Col. Wm. Peachey in 1759. Buckingham Co., Feb. 14, 1780.

Joseph Shores Price, soldier in last French and Indian war under Col. Washington in 1758, one year. Buckingham Co., Mar. 13, 1780.

John Easley, Sergt. in last French and Indian war ; 8 months under Col. Peachey in 1759. Buckingham Co., Feb. 14, 1780.

Peter Roy, soldier in Col. Wm. Peachey's Va. Regt., 8 months in 1759. Buckingham Co., Feb. 14, 1780.

Edmund Peters, Sergt. in Col. Byrd's Regt. under Capt. Thos. Fleming, 8 months in 1758. Buckingham Co., Mar. 13, 1780.

Wm. Northcut, soldier in last French and Indian war ; 8 months under Col. Byrd. Buckingham Co., Mar. 13, 1780.

Thos. Godfrey, soldier in last French and Indian war under Capt. Scott in 1760. Buckingham Co., Mar. 13, 1780.

Benj. Goss, in last French and Indian war under Col. Byrd, 4 months in 1761. Buckingham Co., Mar. 13, 1780.

Asaph Walker, soldier 6 months in last French and Indian war under Col. Byrd. Buckingham Co., Mar. 13, 1780.

Saml. Connor, served in the old Va. Regt. in last war as a soldier. Botetourt Co., Apr., 1780.

Jno. Edwards, soldier in Capt. Mercer's Co. of Regulars, 1st Va. Regt. in last war. Botetourt Co., Apr., 1780.

John Tygert, soldier in old Va. Regt. in last war. Botetourt Co., Apr., 1780.

George Speake, subaltern in the Va. Regt. entitled to 2000 acres of land agreeable to King's Proc. of 1763. Williamsburg, Apr. 21, 1774. Dunmore.

James Alcorn, soldier in Capt. Wm. Preston's Co. of Rangers raised under Act of Assembly in 1759. Montgomery Co., Apr., 1780.

Moses McCann, soldier about 6 months in the additionals to the 1st Va. Regt. during Cherokee expedition in 1760. Montgomery Co., May, 1780.

Philip Watkins, soldier in Capt. John Montgomery's Co. of Vols. incorporated with part of the Va. Regt. in 1756 under Major Lewis, to the end of the expedition. Montgomery Co., Apr., 1780.

Robert Campbell, soldier in Capt. Wm. Christian's Co. of Regulars under command of Col. Byrd till end of campaign. Also soldier in Capt. Blagg's Co. of Regulars in Col. Stephen's Va. Regt. at Fredericksburg in 1762 till same was disbanded. Montgomery Co., Apr., 1780.

Mordecai Buckner, entitled to 3,000 acres of land agreeable to King's Proc. of 1763. Dec. 16, ——. Dunmore.

John Williams, soldier in 1st Va. Regt. commanded by Col. Wm. Byrd in last war. James City Co., Nov. 8, 1779.

James Rion, Jacob Huts, Thos. Ealey and Chas. Suter, soldiers under command of Col. Byrd in last war. (Signed) Abrm. Buford, Col., Petersburg, Oct. 25, 1779. Proved by James Buford in James City Co., Nov. 8, 1779.

Simon Gillet, regular soldier in last war, entitled to land under King's Proc. of 1763. Oct. 26, 1779.

David Poe, regular soldier in last war, entitled to land under King's Proc. of 1763. Oct. 26, 1779.

Jno. Buford, Sergt. in Capt. John Field's Co. Col. Byrd's Regt. (Signed) Thos. Ridley, Major; Petersburg. Oct. 26, 1779. John Buford, heir-at-law of John. Proved by James Buford in James City Co., Nov. 8, 1779.

Henry Bolton, soldier in one of the Va. Regts. in 1758; in Capt. Hancock Eustace's Co. Genl. Crt., Williamsburg, Oct. 21, 1779.

Thos. Poe, soldier in 1st Va. Regt, in last war under command of Col. Wm. Byrd. James City Co., Nov. 8, 1779.

Wm. Hughes produced commission from Fras. Fauquier, Esq., formerly Gov. of Va., dated June 8, 1762, appointing him Adjutant of Col. Adam Stephen's Regt., and another commission from said Fauquier dated May 22, same year, appointing him Lieut. in said Regt. Genl. Crt., Williamsburg, Oct. 22, 1779.

Wm. Kelley, entitled to land under King's Proc. of 1763 as a soldier. Oct. 22, 1779.

Robt. Johnson, decd., Surgeon, 1st Va. Regt. in last war under command of Col. Wm. Byrd. Died in Frederick Co. Will dated Oct. 6, 1763; Prob. Nov. 1, 1763. Robert Johnson, Jr., heir. Wm. Hughes, executor. James City Co., Nov. 8, 1779.

Alex. Sayer, officer in a company incorporated with a detachment of the Va. Regt. under Maj. Andrew Lewis on two different expeditions in said Colony. Robt. Sayer, son and heir. Montgomery Co., Aug., 1779.

Nimrod Newman, Fifer in the old Va. Regt. under command of Col. Byrd Bedford Co., Sept., 1779.

George Rushea, soldier under Col. Byrd in 1760. Bedford Co., Sept. 1779.

Wm. Shepperson, soldier in late war between Great Britain and France. Henrico Co., Nov., 1779.

Thos. Druggers, soldier among the new levies under the command of Col. Byrd in 1760. Bedford Co., July, 1779.

John Conner, soldier in the old Va. Regt. under Col. Washington in 1755; John Adams and Abiel Mead, soldiers under Col. Byrd in 1760. Bedford Co., Aug. 1779.

Jeremiah Pierce, entitled to 2,000 acres of land under Proc. of 1763. Montgomery Co., Oct., 1779.

Abiel Mead, soldier under Col. Byrd in 1760. Bedford Co., Aug., 1779.

Martin Nalle served in an Independent Corps under Major John Field in 1764 in an expedition under Col. Bouquet against the Shawnee Indians. Culpeper Co., Oct. 18, 1779.

Turner Richardson, Sergt. in the late war. Williamsburg, Apr. 5, 1774. Dunmore.

Matthew Anderson, Sergt. under Col. John Hickman in the war between Great Britain and France in 1759. Hanover Co., Oct. 7, 1779.

James Harris, soldier in 2d Va. Regt. in war between Great Britain and France in 1758. Hanover Co., 1779.

Major Genl. Charles Lee, Lieut. in the British service in America in 1755. Lieut. and Capt. of 44th Regt. from 1st campaign in 1755 to total reduction of Canada in 1760; afterwards promoted to rank of Major in 103rd Regt. to close of the war. Frederick Co., Nov. 2, 1779.

James Parish, soldier in one of the Va. Regts. raised during the late war between Gt. Britain and France. Genl. Crt., Oct. 19, 1779.

Ambrose Powell, Captain, signed a discharge August, 1756.

Finley McCoy, entitled to 200 acres of land agreeable to the King's Proc. of 1763. Williamsburg, Feb. 5, 1774. Dunmore.

James Phillips, entitled to 200 acres of land under Proc. of 1763. Feb. 5, 1774. Dunmore.

John Fumace, soldier in Capt. Hogg's Co. of Rangers in 1758. John Fumace, son of John. Orange Co., Oct. 28, 1779.

David Thompson, soldier in Col. Wm. Byrd's Regt. in 1758. Orange Co., Aug. 26, 1779.

Isaac Crosthwait, served full enlistment in Col. Byrd's Regt. in 1758. Orange Co., Oct. 28, 1779.

Wm. Vaughan, Sergt. in Capt. Hogg's Co. of Rangers in 1758. Orange Co., Oct. 28, 1779.

Capt. Jos. Fox, commission appointing him Capt. by Robert Dinwiddie, Esqr. He raised a company and defended the frontiers in the late French and Indian war, until he was discharged. Louisa Co., Oct. 11, 1779.

Thos. Lemen, Lieut. in Capt. Wm. Cox's Co. of Rangers in campaigns of 1756 and 1757. Certificate from Adam Stephen, a Col. of one of the Va. Regts. of Regulars. Genl. Crt., Williamsburg, Oct. 3, 1779.

Samuel Thomas, entitled to 200 acres of land as a Corporal in the late war, agreeable to Proc. of 1763. Williamsburg, May 13, 1774. Dunmore.

Matthew Rowbottom, deceased, soldier in Col. Adam Stephen's Regiment, Capt. Thos. Bullett's Co., in late war between Great Britain and France. General Court, Oct. 29, 1779.

William Armstrong, Corporal in Co. of Rangers under Capt. Peter Hogg, late war between Great Britain and France. General Court, Oct. 28, 1779.

John Lea, soldier in Capt. Christian's Co. of Rangers in 1760 in last war, until legally discharged. Louisa Co., Oct. 11, 1779.

Thomas Swearengen, entitled to 2,000 acres of land agreeable to Proc. of 1763. Williamsburg, Feb. 5, 1774. Dunmore.

John Rosser, entitled to 200 acres of land agreeable to Proc. of 1763. Feb. 5, 1774. Dunmore.

John Chism, soldier in 1758 under Capt. John Field in Genl. Forbes' expedition on the frontiers against the French and Indians. Culpeper Co., Oct. 18, 1779.

Henry Nixon, soldier in 1758 under Capt. John Field, in Genl. Forbes' expedition on the frontiers against the French and Indians. Culpeper Co., Oct. 18, 1779.

Philip Ross, Lieut. of an Independent Co. in Col. Bouquet's expedition against the Shawnee Indians in 1764. General Court, Oct. 26, 1779.

Charles Lewis, deceased, Captain 1st Va. Regt. during the last war. On oath of Gen. George Weedon. Joseph Jones, Esqr., guardian of John and Charles Lewis, sons of said Charles Lewis, deceased. Spotsylvania Co., Oct. 21, 1779.

Moses Collier, soldier in regular service in Col. Byrd's regiment. Rockbridge Co., Aug. 15, 1779.

James Johnson, Sergt. in Capt. Jno. Roote's Co. of Regulars, which company was part of one of the Va. Regts. in 1758. General Court, Oct. 21, 1779.

Jesse May, soldier in one of the Va. Regts. raised during the late war between Great Britain and France. Certificate from Thos. Bullett, a Capt. in that regiment. General Court, Oct. 19, 1779.

Wm. Stewart Packett, Sergt. in one of the Va. Regts. raised during the late war between Great Britain and France. Certificate from Thos. Bullett, a Capt. in one of the said regiments. General Court, Oct. 19, 1779.

Charles Tomkies (Tompkins?) served in 2d Va. Regt. of Regulars, late war between Great Britain and France, as either a Lieut. or Ensign. Certf. from Wm. Peachey, Esqr., a field officer in said regiment. General Court, Oct. 19, 1779.

James Mills, soldier in one of the Va. Regts. during the late war between Great Britain and France. Certificate from Thos. Bullett, a Capt. in one of the said Va. Regts. General Court, Oct. 19, 1779.

Joseph Annet, soldier in one of the Va. Regts. during the late war between Great Britain and France. Certificate from Thos. Bullett, a Capt. in one of the said regiments. General Court, Oct. 19, 1779.

James Jones, entitled to 2,000 acres of land agreeable to King's Proc. of 1763. (No date. Dunmore's signature torn off).

Larkin Chew, Lieut. in Col. Byrd's Va. Regt., entitled to 2,000 acres of land agreeable to King's Proc. of 1763. Jan. 27, 1774.

Henry Bowles enlisted in Col. Byrd's Regt. of Regulars, raised during the late war between Great Britain and France, and served till legally discharged. Chesterfield Co., May 5, 1780.

John Rudd enlisted in Col. Byrd's Regt. of Regulars raised during the late war between Great Britain and France, and served until legally discharged. Chesterfield Co., May 5, 1780.

Benj. Gipson enlisted in Col. Byrd's Regt. of Regulars raised during the late war between Great Britain and France, and served until legally discharged. Chesterfield Co., May, 1780.

Wm. Blankinship enlisted in Col. Byrd's Va. Regt. of Regulars raised during the late war between Great Britain and France, and served until legally discharged. Chesterfield Co., April 7, 1780.

Haly Talbott, Sergt. in 1760 in Col. Byrd's Regt. of Regulars, and served until legally discharged. Chesterfield Co., April 7, 1780.

James Taylor, soldier under Capt. Chas. Scott, who was under command of Col. Wm. Byrd in the expedition against the Indians in 1760, and served until legally discharged. Pittsylvania Co., Mar. 21, 1780.

Wm. Ragsdale, soldier in Capt. John McNeill's Co., under command of Col. Andrew Lewis, in expedition against the Indians in 1760. Served 5 years. Pittsylvania Co., May 16, 1780.

Drury Hudgens, soldier in 1760, and served 6 months in Capt. Charles Scott's Co., Byrd's Regt. Cumberland Co., Mar. 27, 1780.

James Turner, Sergt. in 1758 in 2nd Va. Regiment, commanded by Capt. Hudson, in the late war between Great Britain and France. Goochland Co., Feb. 21, 1780. (Ed. Note). This should be evidently "in company commanded by Capt. Hudson," as Wm. Byrd was commander of 2nd Va. Regt.

Peter Wiley, soldier in Capt. John Dickerson's Co. of Rangers for about 9 months, in the first war. Montgomery Co., May, 1780.

James Acres, soldier in the 1st Va. Regt. of Foot, commanded by Col. Wm. Byrd in 1758 and 1759, for 6 months ; as soon as the six months were up he entered the regiment commanded by Col. Adam Stephen and served as a soldier in same. King and Queen Co., Mar. 13, 1780.

Joseph Newman, soldier in one of the Va. Regts. under command of Genl. Braddock, until properly discharged. Amherst Co., April, 1780.

James Wells, soldier in one of the Va. Regts. in 1760, and served to end of that campaign under command of Col. Wm. Byrd. Amherst Co., Mar., 1780.

James Thompson, soldier in one of the Va. Regts. in 1758, and served under command of Genl. Forbes to end of that campaign. Amherst Co., March, 1780.

James Bridgetts, soldier in 1st Va. Regt. commanded by Col. Wm. Byrd, in late war between Great Britain and France. Augusta Co., Mar. 21, 1780.

John Burton, soldier in 1st Va. Regt., Col. Wm. Byrd commanding, in late war between Great Britain and France. Augusta Co., Mar. 21, 1780.

Wm. Thompson, soldier in the Va. Regts. in 1757, and served to end of the war under the then Col. Washington. Amherst Co., Mar., 1780.

Joseph Willis, soldier in Capt. Dickinson's Co. of Rangers in 1758. Kentucky Co., Feb. 1, 1780.

Wm. Maxwell, Sergt. 35th Regt. in America. Rockbridge Co., May, 1780. (It appears from a discharge to said Maxwell, that his company had served for fifteen years. Henry Fletcher, Lt. Col. 35th Regt. Quebec, Oct. 6, 1757).

John Riley, soldier in the old Va. Regt., commanded by Col. Byrd. Rockbridge Co., May, 1780.

Richard Pouston, entitled to 50 acres of land under Proc. of 1763. Oct. 11, 1774. Dunmore.

Robert Rutherford made oath in 1778, that in 1758 and 1759, Wm. Darke (now a prisoner at New York) served as a Corpl. in a company of Rangers under his command until the same was reduced. Berkeley Co., Mar., 1780.

Robert Buckles, Jr., soldier in company of Rangers commanded by Capt. Robt. Rutherford in 1758, till same was reduced. Berkeley Co., Mar., 1780.

Jervice Sherly, in 1758 or 1759, soldier in a company of Rangers commanded by Capt. Robt. Rutherford, until same was reduced. Berkeley Co., March, 1780.

Geo. Hicks, Sergt. 1755-1761, in a regiment raised for the immediate defense of the state. Caroline Co., Mar., 1780.

Matthew Abbott, Sergt. in Va. Battl. of Regulars, commanded by Col. Wm. Byrd in 1758, until same was discharged. Hanover Co., April 6, 1780.

John Treadway, private in Capt. Nathl. Gist's company of Va. Regt. in last war between Great Britain and France. Charlotte Co., Mar. 6, 1780.

Benj. Cage, private in Capt. Richard Doggett's company of Va. Regt., in last war between Great Britain and France. Charlotte Co., Mar. 6, 1780.

John Ormsby, Esq., commissary in the service of Great Britain in 1758, 1759 and 1760. Yohogania Co., Feb., 1780.

Jeremiah Edwards, soldier in 1st Va. Regt., commanded by Col. Wm. Byrd, in the late war between Great Britain and France. Augusta Co., Mar. 21, 1780.

Wm. Stewart, soldier in Capt. Wm. Preston's company of Rangers in the late war between Great Britain and France in 1758. Augusta Co., Mar. 21, 1780.

Robert Hall, soldier in Capt. Wm. Preston's company of Rangers in the late war between Great Britain and France in 1758. Augusta Co., March 21, 1780.

Joseph Beeler, commander of a company in the last war. Ohio Co., Mar. 7, 1780.

Col. John Buchanan, deceased, Capt. of a company of enlisted men on the frontiers of Augusta from April, 1758, to May, 1759, under immediate command of the then Gov. of Va. James Buchanan, heir-at-law to said Col. B.

Col. James Robertson, subaltern officer in a company of enlisted men before Oct., 1763, under different Captains until whole troops in that quarter were disbanded by order of the Gov. of Va., who had given the command thereof to Col. Andrew Lewis. Montgomery Co., April, 1780.

Wm. Anderson, soldier in Capt. Wm. Preston's company of Rangers from 1758 until May 4, 1759, when the company was disbanded by order of the Govt. Montgomery Co., April, 1780.

John Madison, Capt. of a company of Volunteers by order of the executive power of Va., for the time being on an expedition of which Col. Thomas Nash was chosen to command against the Shawnee Indians in the year 1757. Continued in said service four months when the whole corps composed of several companies of volunteers was disbanded, as the expedition was at an end for which the troops were raised. Montgomery Co., April, 1780.

David Sayers, Sergt. in Capt. Alexr. Sayers' company stationed on the frontiers in 1758. Montgomery Co., May, 1780.

James Board, soldier under command of Col. Byrd in 1761 and 1762. Bedford Co., Mar. 27, 1780.

Archibald Johnson, soldier under Lieut. Benja. Temple in a regular corps raised in Va. in 1759, and also under Capt. John Stears in 1760, which service was against the Indians. Halifax Co., Mar. 16, 1780.

Wm. Griffin, private in Capt. Robert Mumford's company, 1st Va. Regt., in last war between Great Britain and France. Charlotte Co., Mar. 6, 1780.

Roger Cock Bailey, corporal in Capt. James Gunn's company of the Va. Regt. in last war between Great Britain and France. Charlotte Co., Mar. 6, 1780.

David Hutcherson, private in Capt. Posey's company of the Va. Regt in the late war between Great Britain and France. Charlotte Co., Mar., 1780.

John Young, private in Capt. James Gunn' company of 1st Va. Regt. last war between Great Britain and France. Charlotte Co., Mar. 6, 1780.

Humphrey Whayne, Sergt. in a corps raised for defense of Va. in 1755. William Whayne, soldier in the said regiment, both of whom died in the service. Tabitha Whayne made oath that John Whayne is heir-at-law to the said Humphrey and William. King and Queen Co. Court, April ——.

Elisha White, Lieut. in Capt. Joseph Fox's company of Rangers in 1755. Louisa Co., Mar. 13, 1780.

Haynes Morgan, Gent., produced discharge from the 80th British Regt. commanded by Montague Wilmott, Esqr., signed by James Grant, Esqr., Capt. commandant, part of which said regiment was raised in this state in 1758, at which time said Haynes Morgan enlisted, and he was Sergt. Major to said regiment and served 7 years, which said regiment was reduced at New York, 1764. Pittsylvania Co., April 18, 1780.

John Mays, Corporal in the old Va. Regt, in the late war between Great Britain and France. Goochland Co., Feb. 21, 1780.

Moses Barker, non-commissioned officer in the Va. Regt. under my command, entitled to 200 acres under King's Proc. of 1763. March 12, 1774. (Signed) G. Washington.

James Durham, soldier in 1758 and served 6 months under Capt. Robert Rutherford in Byrd's Regt. Cumberland Co., Mar. 27, 1780.

Job Hilliard, soldier in late war, entitled to 50 acres agreeable to Proc. of 1763. Williamsburg, Mar. 3, 1774. Dunmore.

James Colvin, Ensign in a company of Rangers in 1764 in the Va. service in Col. Henry Bouquet's campaign, till legally discharged. Yohogania Co. Court, Feb., 1780.

Joseph Beelor, commanded a company of Rangers in the last war, raised in Va., and was stationed at Fort Cumberland for the defense of the frontier, and continued in said service till said company was recalled and disbanded. Ohio Co., March, 1780.

Isaac McDonald, soldier under Major John McNeill in Col. Adam Stephen's regiment in 1762. Henry Co., March 25, 1780.

Wm. Edlington, entitled to 50 acres of land agreeable to Proc. of r763. March 26, 1774. Dunmore.

David Harfield, non-commissioned officer in late war, entitled to 200 acres of land agreeable to Proc. of 1763. Williamsburg, April 28, 1774. Dunmore.

Jessy Hamblett, entitled to 50 acres of land as a soldier in late war, agreeable to Proc. of 1763. Williamsburg, April 20, 1774. Dunmore.

John Lambeth, Sergt. in last war, entitled to 200 acres of land agreeable to Proc. of 1763. Williamsburg, April 28, 1774. Dunmore.

Henry Townsend, entitled to 50 acres of land agreeable to Proc. of 1763. June 2, 1774. Dunmore.

Jesse Martin, Ensign in the Va. Regiment in 1758. Ohio Co., March, 1780

James Ryan, deceased, soldier, till properly discharged in 1758, in a regiment raised for immediate defense of the state, under Col. Adam Stephen. Caroline Co., March 9, 1780.

Christopher Baltimore, soldier in Capt. Fleming's company under command of Colo. Wm. Peachey in 1758. Fluvanna Co., April 6, 1780.

Benj. Faris, Corporal in Capt. Thomas Flemming's company under command of Colo. Wm. Peachey in 1758. Fluvanna Co., April 6, 1780.

John Marr (or Man) in one of the Va. regiments in last war, died in service. Danl. Man (or Marr) heir-at-law to said John. Fauquier Co., March 27, 1780.

Wm. Smith, now living in Fauquier Co., was a soldier and served 5 or 6 campaigns in 1st Va. Regiment and was wounded near —— in defense of that fort in Oct., 1758. During great part of that time he acted as Sergt. Given under my hand this 2d day of Feb., 1780. (Signed) Adam Stephen, at that time Lt. Col. of the Va. Regiment.

Robert Smith of Prince William Co., enlisted in the 1st Va. Regiment with Lieut. Wright, and that he served in my company as a soldier some considerable time and was afterwards discharged. Given under my hand this 2d day of Feb., 1780. (Signed) Adam Stephen, at that time Lt. Col. of the regiment.

Sam. Daniel, soldier in 1758, till properly discharged, in a regiment raised for the immediate defense of this state. Caroline Co., April, 1780.

Francis Riley, deceased, soldier in Capt. Preston's company of Rangers last war on the frontiers of this colony, till properly discharged. James Rowland, Admr. Botetourt Co., Dec., 1780.

John Pryor, soldier in Capt. Preston's company of Rangers in 1756, 1757 and 1758, till properly discharged. Botetourt Co., April, 1780.

John Taylor, soldier in Capt. Dickinson's company of Rangers on the frontier of Va. last war. Botetourt Co., April, 1780.

James Johnson, soldier in Capt. Throgmorton's company of Regulars last war, till properly discharged. Botetourt Co., April, 1780.

Jno. Reaburne, soldier in Capt. Hogg's company of Rangers last war, till his company was discharged in 1759. Botetourt Co., April, 1780.

James Barnett, Sergt. in Capt. Christian's company of Regulars raised in Va. last war on the Cherokee expedition under command of Col. Byrd, until properly discharged in 1760. Botetourt Co., April, 1780.

Richard Ellis, soldier under Capt. Saml. Meredith in 1758, in Col. Wm. Byrd's regiment, till properly discharged. Richard Ellis, who is so infirm as not to be able to attend Court; Bartlett Ellis made oath to the above. Hanover Co., April 6, 1780.

Ambrose Powell, Gent., Staff officer in defense of this state in 1755, until legally discharged. Orange Co., April 27, 1780.

Wm. Russell, Sergt. under Capt. James Gunn, under command of Col. Wm. Byrd, in the expedition against the Indians in 1760. Pittsylvania Co., March 21, 1780.

Joseph Terry, Sergt. under Capt. Wm. Phillips, who was under the command of Col. Andrew Lewis, in the expedition against the Indians in 1763. Pittsylvania Co., March 21, 1780.

Wm, Terry, soldier under Capt. Joseph Fox, who was under the command of Col. Andrew Lewis, in the expedition against the Indians in 1755. Pittsylvania Co., March 21, 1780.

Wm. Robinson, Lieut. in a company of enlisted men, from July, 1763, to the March following, on the frontiers of Augusta, under command of Capt. Alexr. Sayers, when the company was disbanded by order of Col. Andrew Lewis, who then had command of the troops stationed in Augusta. Montgomery Co., April, 1780.

Col. David Robinson, Lieut. in company of enlisted men under Capt. Alexr. Sayers, from July, 1763, to month of March following, when the company was disbanded by order of Col. Andrew Lewis, who then had command of the troops stationed in Augusta. Montgomery Co., April, 1780.

Francis Smith, Lieut. in a company of enlisted men on the frontier of Augusta Co., from July, 1763, to Dec., 1764, under several captains, and served till troops disbanded. Montgomery Co., April, 1780.

James Dunlop, deceased, Capt. of a company of Rangers raised by Act of Assembly, from June 8, 1757, to Dec. following, being stationed on the frontier by order of the governor of Va., under whose command he was, and he was killed by the savages in 1758, when in the service of his country. James Brown, Adam Gutherie, and George Armstrong, joint-heirs of said James Dunlop, deceased. Montgomery Co., April, 1780.

Thos. Mason, Drummer in the Va. Bat., under command of Wm. Byrd, Esqr., in 1750. Hanover Co., April 6, 1780.

John Crockett, Sergt. in Capt. John Montgomery's company of Volunteers, on the Shawnee expedition in 1756, incorporated with part of the Va. Regt. commanded by Maj. Lewis, continued in said service during the expedition. Montgomery Co., April, 1780.

John Montgomery, Capt., commanded a company of Volunteers, incorporated with part of the Va. Regt. on the Shawnee expedition, under command of Maj. Lewis, continued therein during said expedition. Montgomery Co., April, 1780.

Archibald Buchanan, Sergt. in Capt. Wm. Preston's company of Rangers, about 10 months in 1756 and 1757, until legally discharged. Montgomery Co., April, 1780.

Wm. Carvin, soldier in Capt. John Montgomery's company of Volunteers, incorporated with part of the Va. Regt. in 1756, under Maj. Lewis, and continued therein until end of the expedition. He (Carvin) also served as Sergt. in Capt. Wm. Christian's company, stationed on the frontiers, from July, 1763, to March, 1764, when he was legally discharged. Montgomery Co., April, 1780.

Wm. Sayers, Ensign in a company of men stationed on the frontiers, commanded by Capt. John Buchanan from April, 1758, to May, 1759. Montgomery Co., April, 1780.

John Alsup, soldier, was in the Va. Regt. about three years and was legally discharged when Col. Adam Stephen commanded. Montgomery Co., May, 1780.

James Adams, soldier in Capt. John Smith's company of Regulars, additional troops on the Cherokee expedition in 1760, continued till end of campaign. Montgomery Co., April, 1780.

John Alcorn, soldier in the regular additional troops to the 1st Va. Regt., during the Cherokee expedition, 1760, commanded by Col. Wm. Byrd, being about six months, and also in Capt. John Smith's company. Montgomery Co., May, 1780.

Wm. Tinsley, soldier in Va. Regt., commanded by Col. Byrd, till legally discharged. King William Co., Feb. 16, 1780.

James McCollister, Lieut. in the Penna. Regt. in 1763, in which capacity he served during the late French war. Frederick Co., March, 1780.

Saml. Watts, soldier in 1st Va. Regt., under Capt. Thos. Bullitt, in last war. Halifax Co., April 21, 1780.

Henry Francis, Sergt. 1st Va. Regt., under different commanders, and continued in said service about six and one-half years, at which time he was legally discharged by Col. Adam Stephen. Montgomery Co., May, 1780.

Robt. Stanton, soldier, 2 years in 1st Va. Regt., commanded by Col. Byrd. Montgomery Co., May, 1780.

John Maxey, soldier in last French and Indian war, and continued a soldier till legally discharged by Col., now Gen. Washington, in 1756. Powhatan Co., April 20, 1780.

Joseph Montgomery, soldier in Capt. John Montgomery's company of Volunteers, incorporated in part of the Va. Regt. on the Shawnee expedition in 1756, commanded by Major Lewis, till legally discharged. Montgomery Co., April, 1780.

John Hays, soldier in 1st Va. Regt. about two years, when Col. Stephen commanded it, till legally discharged. Montgomery Co., May, 1780.

Edwd. Cochran, soldier upwards of three years in 1st Va. Regt., under different commanders. Montgomery Co., May, 1780.

Thos. Barker, soldier for nearly seven years under different commanders. Montgomery Co., May, 1780.

John Francis, deceased, soldier in 1st Va. Regt., commanded by Col. Washington, and continued in said service about three years, at which time he was killed by the Indians. Henry Francis, eldest brother and heir of said John Francis, deceased. Montgomery Co., May, 1780.

Wm. Francis, deceased, soldier for three years in the 1st Batt. of Royal Americans, in which service he died. Henry Francis, eldest brother and heir of said Wm. Francis, deceased. Montgomery Co., May, 1780.

Joseph McClung, Sergt., under command of Col. Byrd, against the Cherokee Indians in 1760. Greenbrier Co., March 21, 1780.

John Reyley, soldier in one of the old Va. Regts. under command of Maj. Andrew Lewis. Greenbrier Co., April 19, 1780.

Wm. Scott, Drummer in 1st Va. Regt. Greenbrier Co., March 21, 1780.

James Shaw, soldier in Capt. Peter Hogg's company of Rangers in 1757. Greenbrier Co., April 19, 1780.

Thos. McCauley, Corpl. 2d Va. Regt. in late war between Great Britain and France. Albemarle Co., April 13, 1780.

Henry Davis, soldier in 2d Va. Regt. in war between Great Britain and France. Albemarle Co., April 13, 1780.

Benj. Henslie, Lieut. in Va. Batt., in 1760; certificate from Col. Wm. Byrd. Henry Co., Aug., 1779.

John Hern, soldier in the last war between Great Britain and France, in Capt. James Walker's company, Col. Byrd's Regt., till legally discharged. Mecklenberg Co., May 8, 1780.

Saml. Miller, soldier in one of the Va. Regts. under command of late Wm. Byrd in last war between Great Britain and France. Amherst Co., Feb. 7, 1780.

Francis Lightfoot, Sergt , in last war between Great Britain and France, Col. Mercer's company, 2d Va. Regt. Mecklenberg Co., May 8, 1780.

Joseph Lambert, soldier in company commanded by Maj. Stewart, Col. Adam Stephen's Regt., in late war between Great Britain and France, till properly discharged. Mecklenburg Co., May 8, 1780.

Thos. Foster, soldier in Col. Buchanan's company, stationed on the frontier in 1758 and 1759, till legally discharged. Montgomery Co., April, 1780.

Augustine Broomley, soldier in Capt. Blagg's company till legally discharged. Botetourt Co., March 9, 1780.

David Fream, soldier in Capt. Christian's company of Regulars in last war, till legally discharged. Botetourt Co., Dec., 1779.

Robert Hutcheson, Sergt. in Capt. Claiton's company, Pennsylvania Regulars, last war, at the reduction of Fort Pitt. Botetourt Co., March, 1780.

Joshua Cox, soldier in Capt. John Smith's company of Regulars on the expedition of 1760, under command of Col. Byrd; served to end of campaign. Montgomery Co., April, 1780.

Hugh McNeill, Drummer in Capt. Throgmorton's company in old Va. Regt., till legally discharged. Botetourt Co., March, 1780.

Julius Webb, soldier in Capt. Throgmorton's company of Regulars in old Va. Regt. till legally discharged. Botetourt Co., March, 1780.

John Plumb (or Plumbly), soldier in Capt. Christian's company of Regulars, last war. Botetourt Co., March, 1780.

James Cooper, soldier in Capt. Gist's company of Light Infantry in last war. Botetourt Co., March, 1780.

William Holley, soldier in Capt. Christopher Gist's company of Light Infantry in last war, till legally discharged. Botetourt Co., March, 1780.

Peter Brannan, served in Capt. Stewart's company of Regulars in last war, till legally discharged. Botetourt Co., March, 1780.

John Bowyer, entitled to 2,000 acres of land, agreeable to proclamation of 1763. Williamsburg, April 20, 1774. Dunmore.

Edmund Bacon, entitled to 200 acres of land as Corporal in last war, agreeable to proclamation of 1763. Williamsburg, May 29, 1774. Dunmore.

John Haynes, soldier in Capt. Throgmorton's company of Regulars in last war, till legally discharged. Botetourt Co., March, 1780.

William Davis, soldier in Capt. Dickinson's company of Rangers in 1758. Kentucky Co., Feb. 1, 1780.

Thos. Miller, soldier in Capt. Christian's company of Rangers in 1756, till legally discharged. Botetourt Co., March, 1780.

Archibald Lockhart enlisted in the 1st Va. Regt. in 1752. Kentucky Co., Feb. 1, 1780.

James Davis, soldier in Col. Byrd's Regt. in 1761. Kentucky Co., Feb. 1, 1780.

Nicholas Branstone, entitled to 200 acres of land for services in last war, agreeable to proclamation of 1763. Williamsburg, Feb. 9, 1774. Dunmore.

Barney Ryley, soldier in 1st Va. Regt., and continued therein until reduction thereof. Kentucky Co., Feb. 1, 1780.

Henry Cremore, entitled to 50 acres of land as a soldier in the last war, agreeable to proclamation of 1763. Williamsburg, April 26, 1774. Dunmore.

Saml. Meredith, Capt. in the Va. Regt. under command of Col. Byrd, entitled to 3,000 acres of land, agreeable to proclamation of 1763. Williamsburg, March 9, 1774. Dunmore.

Wm. Haymand, Sergt. in the old Va. Regt.; certificate from Col. Adam Stephen. Monongalia Co., Nov., 1779.

Robert Mennis, soldier under Capt. Wm. Christian, in Col. Wm. Byrd's Regt. Rockingham Co., March 28, 1780.

Jacob Pence soldier in Capt. Hogg's company of Rangers from 1757 until they were discharged at Bedford. Rockingham Co., March 28, 1780.

Thos. Dalley served in a Regt. in which Thos. Elliott was a commissioned officer ; certificate from Thos. Elliott, above mentioned. John Dalley, heir-at-law. Essex Co., March 20, 1780.

John Stephenson, soldier in Capt. McClanahan's Independent company, in Col. Bouquet's campaign, till legally discharged. Rockingham Co., March, 1780.

David Laird, Corpl. in Capt. Hogg's company of Rangers in 1757, until it was discharged at Bedford. Rockingham Co., March 28, 1780.

Lieut. Alex. McDonald, entitled to 2,000 acres of land for services in the late war, agreeable to proclamation of 1763. Williamsburg, March 3, 17——. Dunmore.

Hugh Stephenson, entitled to 3,000 acres of land, agreeable to proclamation of 1763. Williamsburg, May 16, 1774. Dunmore.

Dr. James Craik, Lieut. in Va. Regt. commanded by Col. Wm. Byrd, entitled to 2,000 acres of land, agreeable to proclamation of 1763. 5th day of Oct., 1773. Dunmore.

Geo. Teator, soldier in Capt. Gist's company of Regulars, 1st Va. Regt., last war, till legally discharged. Botetourt Co., Dec., 1779.

Solomon Simpson, Edward Gill, Sr., Christopher Finnie, Christopher Best, and Wm. Cross, soldiers in the 1st. Va. Regt., last war, under command of Col. Byrd and Col. Stephens. Botetourt Co., Dec., 1779.

William Leather, soldier in Capt. Bullitt's old Va. Regt., last war. Botetourt Co., Feb., 1780.

Wm. Simpson, deceased, soldier in 1st Va. Regt., under Col. Washington, till he (said Wm.) departed this life. Solomon Simpson, heir-at-law. Botetourt Co., Feb., 1780.

John Collins, soldier in Capt. Christian's company of Rangers in 1760, on expedition commanded by Col. Byrd, against Cherokee Indians. Botetourt Co., Dec., 1779.

William Ward, Lieut. in Capt. Breckenridge's company of Rangers, which was incorporated with a detachment of the 1st Va. Regt. in 1760, on expedition commanded by Col. Byrd against the Cherokee Indians. Botetourt Co., Feb., 1780.

John Turnley, soldier in Capt. Christian's company of Rangers in 1760, on expedition commanded by Col. Byrd against the Cherokee Indians. Botetourt Co., Dec., 1779.

Wm. Gill, deceased, soldier in old Va. Regt., until he departed this life. Edwd. Gill, heir-at-law. Botetourt Co., Feb., 1780.

John Anthony, deceased, Capt. of a company of Rangers in 1759, by particular order of the Governor and under commission from him. John Anthony, heir-at-law. Bedford Co., March, r780.

John Wright, soldier under Col. Byrd in 1758, and was then discharged. Bedford Co., March, 1780.

Justinian Wills, Sergt.-Maj. under Col. Byrd in 1758. Bedford Co., March, 1780.

David Crews, Corporal in 1760 under Col. Byrd. Bedford Co., March, 1780.

James Noland, soldier under Col. Washington in 1755, and under Col. Byrd in 1762. Bedford Co., March, 1780.

George Rice, staff officer in Bouquet's expedition to the westward, in the late war between Great Britain and France. Frederick Co., March 8, 1780.

Wm. Hughes, entitled to 2,000 acres of land under King's Proclamation of 1763, he having served as a Lieut. in the Va. Regt. May 20, 1774. Dunmore.

Alex. Waugh, Jr., Staff Officer for the Va. forces under Col. Byrd in 1758. Culpeper Co., April 17, 1780.

Charles Sims, Gent., produced in Court a commission from Francis Bernard, Esq., formerly governor of New Jersey, dated March 15, 1759, appointing Wm. Douglas, Maj. of a Regt. in that Province, whereof the Hon. Peter Schuyler was Col. He also produced the affidavit of Rev. David Griffith, taken before Wm. Ramsey, Esqr., a Justice of the Peace for Fairfax Co., that Wm. Douglas, commonly called Major, who formerly resided on Staten Island, did serve as an officer in the corps of the Provincials raised by New Jersey in the late war between Great Britain and France. George Beardmore served as a soldier in campaign with said Douglas in the late war of Great Britain with France. Prince William Co., April 4, 1780.

Michael Counsel, entitled to 50 acres of land, agreeable to the King's Proclamation of 1763. April 1, 1774. Dunmore.

James McGavock, Capt. of a company of Volunteers on an expedition against the Shawnees, Col. Thos. Nash, commander, in 1757. Continued in said service four months, when whole corps was disbanded. Montgomery Co., April 6, 1780.

Nathan Wheelon, Corporal in 2d Va. Regt. in late war between Great Britain and France. Goochland Co., April 17, 1780.

Sherwood Strong, deceased, soldier in late war between Great Britain and France. Sworn to by John Strong. Goochland Co., Sept. 21, 1779.

James Wilkinson, soldier 2d Va. Regt., late war between Great Britain and France. Goochland Co., Feb. 21, 1780.

Ludwick Shadow, deceased, Sergt. under command of Col. Henry Bouquet, in late war between Great Britain and France. Discharge signed by said Bouquet, Nov. 5, 1762. Augusta Co., March 22, 1780.

Robert Ross, soldier in late war in expedition commanded by Col Bouquet. Augusta Co., March 22, 1780.

Wm. Skillern, Ensign in Capt. Robt. Breckenridge's company, raised in Augusta Co., by order of Col. Wm. Byrd, to garrison Ft. Chiswell in the absence of the army on the expedition against the Cherokees in 1760, and continued in the same till legally discharged. Botetourt Co., April, 1780.

John Norris, soldier in old Va. Regt., last war, till legally discharged. Botetourt Co., April, 1780.

John Young, soldier in Va. Regt. three years under Col. Byrd, till legally discharged. Montgomery Co., April, 1780.

Michael Van Buskirk, Ensign to a Company of Foot in the Maryland Service, commanded by Capt. Alexander Beale. Entitled to 2,000 acres of land, agreeable to the King's Proclamation of 1763. March 19, 1774, commission from Gov. Sharp, of Md., to said Buskirk, dated May 2, 1756, to be Ensign in a corps raised by Alex. Beale, for the service of Md. Yohogania Co., Dec., 1779.

James Melliory, soldier in the last war in Capt. Posey's Regular Co., till legally discharged. Botetourt Co., March, 1780.

Israel Christian, served in 1759 as commissary to the Battl. commanded by Col. Peachey till legally disbanded, and afterwards occasionally for the troops of the 1st Va. Regt. in last war. Botetourt Co., April, 1780.

Peter Looney, decd., Sergt. in Capt. Smith's Co. of Rangers last war, till he was taken prisoner by the French and Indians in 1756. That he did not return from his captivity for near two years. Peter Looney, heir-at-law. Botetourt Co., March, 1780.

John Tatham, Sergt. in Capt. Stewart's Co. of Regulars, raised in Va. for the 1st Va. Regt., commanded by Col. Byrd, till legally discharged. Botetourt Co., April, 1780.

James Doreus, soldier in Capt. Woodward's Co. of Regulars, last war, till legally discharged. Botetourt Co., March, 1780.

Charles Ellison, Corpl. in Capt. Roote's Co. of Regulars last war, till legally discharged, Botetourt Co., April, ——.

William Hutcheson, soldier in Capt. Preston's Co. of Rangers in 1759, till it was legally discharged. Botetourt Co., April, 1780.

Peter Wiley, soldier in Catp. Dickerson's Co. of Rangers last war, till legally discharged. Botetourt Co., April, 1780.

John Wiley, soldier in Capt. Dickerson's Co. of Rangers in last war, till legally discharged. Botetourt Co., April, 1780.

John Codare, soldier in Capt. Wm. Preston's Co. of Rangers, from the fall of 1755 to June, 1756. Israel Christian, representative of said Codare. Montgomery Co., April, 1780.

Alexr. Gillespie, soldier in Capt. Chas. Lewis' Co. of Rangers in the late war in 1758. Augusta Co., March, 21, 1780.

Chas. Smith, Sergt. in Capt. Wm. Preston's Co. of Rangers in the late war between Great Britain and France. Augusta Co., March 21, 1780.

Saml. Allen, Capt. in Col. Wyser's Regt. in Penna.; also a Capt. in Col. Byrd's Regt. in 1760. Henry Co., April 27, 1780.

Matthew Small, soldier under Capt. Wm. Christian in Col. Byrd's Regt. in 1760. Henry Co., March, 24, 1780.

Moses Going, soldier under Capt. James Gunn in Col. Byrd's Regt. in 1760. Henry Co., April 27, 1780.

Francis Posey, soldier under Col. Adam Stephen in 1762. Henry Co., April 27, 1780.

Thos. Earles, Sergt. under Capt. Gist in Col. Byrd's Regt. in 1760. Henry Co., April 27, 1780.

Wm. Bartee, Sergt. under Capt. John Smith in Col. Byrd's Regt. in 1760. Henry Co., March 24, 1780.

John Acuts, Sergt. under Capt. Robt. Munford in Col. Byrd's Regt. in 1760.

Henry Austin, entitled to 200 acres of land as Sergt. in the late war, agreeable to Proc. of 1763. Williamsburg, April 27, 1774. Dunmore.

John Brown, entitled to 200 acres of land as a Corpl. in the late war, agreeable to Proc. of 1763. Williamsburg, April 28, 1774. Dunmore.

John Gunnell, soldier in Capt. Temple's Co. of Rangers in Col. Byrd's Regt. in 1758. Louisa Co., April 11, 1780.

David Hudson, soldier in 2d Va. Regt. in the late war between Great Britain and France. Goochland Co., Sept., 1779.

Joseph Bickley, Lieut. in Capt. Wm. Phillip's Co. of Vol. Rangers in 1763. Said Joseph is dead and Joseph Bickley is his heir-at-law. Louisa Co., Feb. 14, 1780.

John Bethel, soldier in 1st Va. Regt., commanded by Col. Washington, about 6 months. Montgomery Co., May, 1780.

David Davies, soldier in Capt. John Montgomery's Co. of Vols. during the Shawnee expedition in 1756, commanded by Major Lewis. Robt. Montgomery representative of said David Davies. Montgomery Co., April, 1780.

Saml. Davies, soldier in Capt. John Montgomery's Co. of Vols. in the Shawnee expedition in 1756, commanded by Major Lewis. Montgomery Co., April, 1780.

John Adams, Sergt. in Capt. John Smith's Co. of Regulars in the Cherokee expedition in 1760, under Col. Byrd's command. Montgomery Co., April, 1780.

Saml. Montgomery, soldier in Capt. Jno. Montgomery's Co. of Vols. in the Shawnee expedition in 1756, commanded by Major Lewis. Montgomery Co., April, 1780.

Alexr. Page, soldier in 1st Va. Regt., about 3 years, under command of Col. Stephen. Montgomery Co., May, 1780.

Israel Christian, Capt. of a Co. of Vols., by order of the executive power of Va., on an expedition of which Col. Thos. Nash was commander against the Shawnees in 1757. Montgomery Co., May, 1780.

Wm. Davis, Sergt. in Capt. Wm. Preston's Co. of Rangers from July, 1755, until June, 1756, and also Sergt. in sd. Preston's 2d. Co. of Rangers about 9 months, in 1758-9. Montgomery Co., April, 1780.

Wm. Montgomery, Sr., soldier in Capt. John Montgomery's Co. of Vols. incorporated with part of the Va. Regt., under command of Major Lewis, on the Shawnee expedition of 1756. Montgomery Co., April, 1780.

James Buchanan, decd., Lieut. in Capt. Alexander's Co. of Vols. on an expedition against the Shawnees, in 1756, with Col. Thos. Nash commander. Continued in same about 4 months, until whole corps, consisting of several companies of Vols., was disbanded. Montgomery Co., May, 1780.

James Milligan, soldier in Capt. Hogg's Ranging Co., in 1754 until disbanded. Greenbrier Co., March 21, 1780.

James Lockhart, soldier in Capt. Alexr. Sayer's Co. of Rangers before 1763, until discharged. Greenbrier Co., March 21, 1780.

Wm. Hamilton, soldier in Capt. John Dickson's (Dickerson's?) Co. of Rangers in 1758 and 1759, until same was discharged. Greenbrier Co., March 21, 1780.

Chas. Poor, soldier in the Va. Regt. under Col. Byrd, sometime in year 1759. Westmoreland Co., Feb., 1780.

George Mothershead, soldier in 2d Va. Regt. under Col. Byrd, in 1759. Westmoreland Co., March, 1780.

Wm. Wright, Wm. Provo, Vincent Rollins and Robt. Sherington, soldiers in 2d Va. Regt. in Capt. Hancock Eustace's Co., of which I was Lieut. during the campaign of 1750. (Signed) Chas. Mynn Thurston, Frederick Co., Oct. 11, 1774.

Thos. Shiflett, soldier in 2d Va. Regt. in late war between Great Britain and France. Albemarle Co., April 13, 1780.

Edwd. Wilkerson, entitled to 200 acres of land as Sergt. in late war, agreeble to Proc. of 1763. Williamsburg, April 28, 1774. Dunmore.

Edmond Bacon, entitled to 200 acres of land as Corpl. in last war, according to Proc. of 1763. Williamsburg, May 29, 1774. Dunmore.

John Bowyer, entitled to 2,000 acres of land, agreeable to Proc. of 1763. Williamsburg, April 20, 1774. Dunmore.

Peter Brannan, served in Capt. Stewart's Co. of Rangers last war as —— until properly discharged. Botetourt Co., March, 1780.

William Holly, soldier in Capt. Gist's Co. of Light Infantry last war, till properly discharged. Botetourt Co., March, 1780.

Robt. Hutcheson, Sergt. in Capt. Claiton's Co. of Penna. Regulars last war at the reduction of Fort Pitt. Botetourt Co., March, 1780.

David Fream, soldier in Capt. Christian's Co. of Regulars in last war, till properly discharged. Botetourt Co., Dec., 1779.

Augustine Bromley, soldier in Capt. Blagg's Regular Co. last war, till properly discharged. Botetourt Co., March 9, 1780.

James Cooper, soldier in Capt. Gist's Co. of Light Infantry last war, till properly discharged. Botetourt Co., March, 1780.

Julius Webb, soldier in Capt. Throgmorton's Co. of Regulars in last war, till properly discharged. Botetourt Co., March, 1780.

Joshua Cox, soldier in Capt. John Smith's Co. of Regulars in expedition of 1760, under command of Col. Byrd, till end of campaign. Montgomery Co., April, 1780.

Richard Janet, entitled to 200 acres of land, agreeable to Proc. of 1763. Williamsburg, Feb. 14, 1774. Dunmore.

Saml. Hamilton, entitled to 200 acres of land for services as Sergt, agreeable to King's Proc. of 1763. Williamsburg, Jan. 31, 1774. Dunmore.

Patrick Miller, soldier in late war between Great Britain and France in Capt. Wm. Preston's Co. of Rangers in 1758. Augusta Co., Feb. 15, 1780.

Benj. Row, entitled to 50 acres of land under King's Proc. of 1763. Jan., 1774. Dunmore.

John Kinkead, soldier in late war in Capt. Wm. Preston's Co. of Rangers, in 1758. Augusta Co., Feb. 15, 1780.

Wm. Jackson, soldier in late war in Capt. Wm. Preston's Co. of Rangers, in 1758. Augusta Co., Feb. 15, 1780.

Lofftus Pullen, soldier in late war in Capt. Wm. Preston's Co. of Rangers, in 1758. Augusta Co., Feb. 15, 1780.

Robert Gwinn, soldier in late war in Capt. Wm. Preston's Co. of Rangers, in 1758. Augusta Co., Feb. 15, 1780.

John Carlile, soldier in late war in Capt. Wm. Preston's Co. of Rangers, in 1758. Augusta Co., Jan. 10, 1780.

Wm. Black, soldier in late war in Capt. Wm. Preston's Co. of Rangers, 1758. Augusta Co., Feb. 15, 1780.

Thos. Hicklin, soldier in late war in Capt. Wm. Preston's Co. of Rangers, in 1758. Augusta Co., Feb. 15, 1780.

Robt. Graham, decd., soldier in late war in Capt. Wm. Preston's Co. of Rangers in 1758. Major Andrew Lockridge, guard. of orphans of Robt. Graham, decd. Augusta Co., Feb. 15, 1780.

Thomas Kinkead, soldier in late war in Capt. Lewis' Co. in the expedition commanded by Col. Bouquet, in 1764. Augusta Co., Feb. 15, 1780.

Wm. Kinkead, soldier in late war in Capt. Lewis' Co. in the expedition commanded by Col. Bouquet, in 1764. Augusta Co., Feb. 15, 1780.

Stephen Handcock, soldier in Col. Byrd's Regt. in 1760. Kentucky Co., Feb. 1, 1780.

Uriah Humphries, soldier in last war in Capt. Posey's Co. of Regulars, till properly discharged. Botetourt Co., March, 1780.

John Nixon, entitled to 200 acres of land as a Sergt., agreeable to Proc. of 1763. Williamsburg, April 16, 1774. Dunmore.

William Brock, soldier in Capt. Wm. Phillip's Co. of Rangers, in 1763. Louisa Co., Feb. 14, 1780.

Littleberry Lane, soldier in Col. Byrd's Regt., in 1758. Orange Co., March 23, 1780.

Henry Shackleford, soldier in Capt. Hogg's Co. of Rangers, in 1758. Orange Co., Nov. 25, 1779.

Patrick Fisher, Sergt. in Col. Byrd's Regt. Orange Co., March 23, 1780.

Bartelott Goodman, soldier in Capt. Thos. Bullitt's Co. of Rangers, in 1762. Louisa Co., Nov. 8, 1779.

John Dalton, soldier in Capt. Thos. Bullitt's Co. of Rangers, in 1762. Louisa Co., Nov. 8, 1779.

Peter Clarkson, soldier in campaign of 1755 in Capt. Saml. Overton's Co. of Rangers. Albemarle Co., March, 1780.

Chas. Walls (or Watts), soldier in 1758 in Col. Byrd's Regt. David Wall (or Watts), heir to said Chas. Orange Co., March 23, 1780.

Chas. Pearcy, soldier in Col. Byrd's Regt. in 1759. Orange Co., Feb. 24, 1780.

Jacob Baughman, soldier in 1st Va. Regt. French and Indian Wars. Kentucky Co., Feb. 2, 1780.

Simon Powell, decd., Sergt. in Capt. Hogg's Co. of Rangers. Elizabeth Jennett Head, wife of James Head, and Sally Riddle, wife of Lewis Riddle, co-heiresses of Simon Powell, decd. Orange Co., Dec. 23, 1779.

Achilles Whitlock, decd., soldier in 1758 in a regt. raised for the immediate defense of the state. John Whitlock, eldest son and heir-at-law to said Achilles. Caroline Co., March, 1780.

James Chick, decd., soldier in 1760 in a regt. raised for immediate defense of the state. John Chick, heir-at-law of the said James. Caroline Co., Feb., 1780.

Edward Brown, soldier in 1758 in a regt. raised for immediate defense of this state. Caroline Co., Feb., 1780.

John Powell, soldier in 1758 in a regt. raised for immediate defense of this state. Caroline Co., March, 1780.

George Teater, Sergt. in Col. Byrd's Regt. in 1761. Kentucky Co., Feb. 1, 1780.

Wm. Dun, Corpl. in Va. Regt. under command of Col. Byrd. March 8, 1774. Dunmore.

Martin Hewlett, Corpl. in Va. Regt. under command of Col. Byrd. April 4, 1774. Dunmore.

Wm. Murrell, Sergt. in Va. Regt., entitled to 200 acres under King's Proc. of 1763. Williamsburg, Dec. 16, 1773. Dunmore.

Thos. Mullen, Corpl. in Va. Regt. commanded by Col. Byrd. March 10, 1774. Dunmore.

Alexander Stewart, entitled to 200 acres of land, agreeable to the King's Proc. of 1763. April 1, 1774. Dunmore.

Militia Rosters in Hening's Statutes at Large.

CULPEPER COUNTY, MARCH, 1756.

Wm. Russell, Lieut. Col.
William Brown, Capt.
John Field, Lieut.
Geo. Weatherall, Serj.

Charles Yancey, Ensign
John Strother, Capt.
Francis Strother, Lieut.
William Roberds, Ensign

Stephen Rogers, Serj.
John Gambill, Serj.
Henry Gambill, Serj.
Sallis Hansford, Serj.

Foot Soldiers.

Francis Cooper
Wm. McDaniel
John Thomas
Miles Murfee
John Hayes
John Graham
Joshua Sherald
Wm. Wall
Jacob Browning
Wm. Boworn
John Laton
Rich. Burk
Rich. Parks
Nicholas Yager
Cornelius Mitchell
John Browning
William Tapp
Samuel Moore

John Willhoit
James Gillison
Benj. Morgan
John Shropshire
David Bridges
John Younger
John Bowman
George Goggan
Mordock Mackenzie
Jacob Wall
John Dixon Wright
Daniel Delaney
Alexander Baxter
John Cave
James Nash
Wm. Twiman
Joel Yarborough

Francis Grant
Adam Maland
Adam Barler
John Greson
John Relsback
Andrew Carpenter
Lewis Fisher
John Gloor
Matthias Weaver
Christopher Barler
Timothy Swindele
John Plunketpeter
Matthias Rouce
Wm. Yager
John Grim
Jacob Harroback
Harmer Young
Henry Gaines

Source: Hening, Vol. 7.

FAIRFAX COUNTY, MARCH, 1756.

Lewis Ellzey, Capt.
Sampson Turley, Lieut.
Saml. Tillett, Corp.

James Tillett, Corp.
Sampson Demovill, Corp.
Jerem. Hutchinson, Corp.

Joseph Stephens, Corp.
Philip Grymes, Corp.
Gilbert Simson, Jr., Corp.

Troopers.

Geo. Shortridge
Benj. Ladd
Nathan Williamson
Vincent Boggess
Joseph Fry
Daniel Thomas
Benj. Hutchison

George Simson
Holland Middleton
Thomas Shore
Wm. Southard
Robert Watson, servant
    to Lewis Ellzey
Thos. Simmonds

John Berkley, Junr.
Francis Eaton
William Pickett
Jesse Martin
Charles Newland
Thomas West
John Price

Richard Newall
James Chamberlayne
Thos. Cartwright
David Thanas, Junr.
Edward Davis
Wm. Peake, Junr.
Wm. Trammell
Gilbert Simson, Junr.
Wm. Scutt
Wm. Musgrove
Wm. Hayes

Edward Masterson
Mark Chilton
Thomas Triplett
William Morris
Wm. Smith
John Stephens
Thomas Osborn
Geo. Saunders
Danl. Shoemaker
Joseph Burson
Simon Shoemaker

Edward Hardin
Nicholas Grymes
Michael Regan, Junr.
Wm. Owsley
Joseph Jones
Joseph Martin
Wm. Stackhouse
John Sinclare
David Smith
Clement Gamer
John Dawson

Source: Hening, Vol. 7.

PRINCE WILLIAM COUNTY, MARCH, 1756.

John Frogg, Major
Wm. Baylis, Capt.
Richard Taylor, Lieut.
of Horse
Wm. Splane, Lieut. of
Horse
Wm. Farrow, Cornet

Saml. Porter, Corp.
Jacob Spilman, Corp.
Wm. Whaley, Corp.
Lewis Reno, Corp.
Wm. Buchanan, Corp.
Thomas Foard, Corp.
George Kenner, Corp.

Henry Floid, Serj.
Foushee Tebbs, Capt.
John Baylis, Capt.
James Seaton, Lieut. of
Foot
Richard Hampton, Lieut
of Foot

Troopers.

John Nevill
Rich. Matthews
Benj. Wilson
Stephen Maurice
Thos. Marshall
Rich. Marshall
John Luttrell
Thos. Doyle
Joshua Welch
Nathaniel Freeman
Standley Singleton
Saml. Batson
John Murray

Wm. Fielder
Andrew Cannaird
John McMillon
Henry Kemper
John Fishback
Clement Norman
Joseph Martin
Richard Byrne
Peter Pierce
Michael Lynn
John Cornwell
John Dowell
Wm. Key
Saml. Grigsby

Robt. Nevill
Thos. Gardner
Chas. Smith
Isaac Gibson
Benj. Edwards
John Coreham
Griffin Matthews
John Bland, Junr.
Wm. Peake
Wm. Berry
Gilbert Crupper
Wm. Barr
Nath. Overal

Foot Soldiers.

Nicholas Hill
John Bolling
Edward O'Neil
Joseph Neal
John Carter
Thos. Shirley
Lewis Oden

John Green
Martin Suttle
David Parsons
George Rose
John Low
James Crocket
Wm. Suttle

Wm. Bolling
Isaac Settle
Wm. Jenings
Valentine Barton
Wm. Crouch
Moses Coppage
John Rice

Source: Hening, Vol. 7.

AUGUSTA COUNTY, SEPTEMBER, 1758.

John Buchanan, Colonel   John Brown, Major   John Smith, Major

Captains.

Alex. Sayers	Ephraim Love	John Maxwell
Abraham Smith	Wm. Preston	Andrew Hays
John Buchanan	Wm. Christian	James Dunlop
John Dickenson	Saml. Norwood	Geo. Robinson
Francis Kirtley	David Steuart, Col. (as Capt.)	John Smith

Lieutenants.

Sampson Archer	James Henderson	Alex. Thompson
Wm. Cunningham	Chas. Wilson	Arch. Buchanan
Christian Bingaman	Wm. Lewis	Alex. Hamilton
Danl. Smith	James McDowell	Robt. Rennick
John Hopkins		Edwin Peterson

Ensigns.

James Henderson	—— Cunningham	Audley Paul
John Hopkins	John Matthews	Josiah Wilson
	John Henderson	

Sergeants.

Benj. Kinley	Michael Henderson	James Couden
Wm. Cravens	Peter Looney	John Wardlaw
John McCoy	Benj. Hansley	Alex. Buchanan
Wm. Clark	Robt. Armstrong	Thos. Hudson
John McKay	John Davice	David Gallaway
John Ozban	Matt. Campbell	Edward Howard
John McCay	John Bowin	Thos. Hugart
Jonas Friend		Wm. Edemston

Corporals.

Robt. Tremble	Wm. Mintor	Thos. McCorne
John Jameson	Geo. Malcomb	Thos. Cavon
Thos. Pritchard	Adam Stevenson	John Gay
John Phares		Robt. Lusk

Militia.

Robt. Mitchell	Henry Benningar	Chas. Driver
Wm. Blackwood	Adam Harper	James Anderson
John Black	Woolrey Coonrod	James Young
Rich. Yedley	Wm. Minter	Wm. Rolestone
John Lawn	Wm. Cunningham	Matt. Rolestone
Adam Dunlop	Robt. McCarney	John Peterson
John Cosby	Danl. McKnight	Darby Conway
Robt. McCoy	John Cunningham	Martin Cornet
Andrew Little	Andrew Cunningham, Jr.	Thos. McNamar
Geo. Lewis	Edward Watts	Thos. Peterson

James Fowler
Saml. Semple
Michael Mallow
John Stephenson
John Shill
Matt. Paten
Rich. Wilson
Hugh Diver
Danl. Henderson
James Ramsay
John Johnston
Alex. Craig
John Melcum
Joseph Melcum
Michael Props
Adam Props
Robt. Minice
John McKay
Wm. McGill, Jr.
Wm. McGill, Sr.
Robt. Boyd
Moses Hall
Peter Veneman
John Young
Michael Erhart
Wm. Minter
Rich. Wilson
John Shanklin
Edward Megary
Paul Shever
James McClure
James Fowler
Joseph Skidmore
Nicholas Hoffman
Henry Peninger
Robt. Megary
Henry Smith
John Smith
John Malcom
Larkin Pearpoint
James Gray
Robt. Gragg
Robt. Cunningham
David Smith
Wm. Bratton
Josiah Shipman
Wm. Rolestone
Robt. Trimble
John Stevenson
John Gum
Robert Gibson

John Walker
Christian Clement
Adam Stephenson
John McClure
James Bell
John Long
Wm. McFarland
John Peary
Wm. Black
David Scott
James Steel
Gilbert Christian
James Meeter
James Lockart
John Shields
John Woods
Arthur Trader
Robt. Patterson
Robt. McGeary
Matt. Black
Nathan Harrison
Leonard Herron
Cornelius Sullivant
Edward Shanklin
Hugh Campbell
James Skidmore
Saml. Briggs
Michael Dickey
John Davis
Thos. Nicholas
James Fowler
Arch. Gilkison
John Malcolm
Wm. Elliot
Thos. Spencer
Geo. Jordon
Wm. McHenry
Joseph Jenkins
Danl. Evans
Rich. Shanklin
Wm. Hooks
James Gamble
James Alexander
John Johnson
Thos. Lawrence
James Stephenson
Danl. Remi
John Farrell
Wm. Kite
Adam McCormick
John Leonard

Martin Phillips
Wm. Woods
James Burk
Abram Earhart
John Blor
Geo. Watts
Gasper Smith
Michael Earhart
Nicholas Hufman
Philip Harper
Valentine Castle
Jacob Harper
Geo. Hamer
Jacob Hornbery
Nicholas Frank
Thomas Boyne
Peter Moses
Geo. Moses
Adam Harper
Geo. Mouse
Paul Shaver
Michael Frees
Peter Vanimon
Philip Hufman
Wm. Wilson
Henry Beniger
John Cunrod
John Malcomb
James McClure
John Cunningham
Wm. Mintor
Isiah Shipman
Jacob Peterson
Jacob Wiece
Joseph Wiece
Benj. Hagler
John Hagler
Postine Hagler
Jacob Hagler
John Wizer
Henry Carr
Martin Peterson
Jeremiah Copper
Robt. Trimble
Jacob Goodman
Gabl. Pickins
Wm. Shaw
John Young
Michael Earhart, Jr.
Mathias Tice
Nicholas Sivers

Nicholas Havener
Jacob Aberman
Wm. Dyer
Andrew Full
John Still
Michael Malow
Michael Eberman
John Aberman
Adam Little
Wm. Wilson
Robt. Homes
Danl. Evans
David Lard
Jacob Rolman
Thos. Bowens
Matt. Black
John Crosby, Jr.
Thos. Lawrence
Geo. Goodman
Geo. Capliner
Henry Smith
Michael Hogshead
John Crosby, Sr.
William Cunningham
John Young
Wm. Flemin
Robt. Cunningham
Thos. McComb
Rich. Wilson
Wm. Gragg
Thos. Paterson
Robt. Magery
Joseph Dixton
Wm. Woods
Danl. Reme
Geo. Hedrick
John Seller
John Miller
Chas. Man
Jacob Pence
Jacob Grub
Chas. Rush
Conrad Kinsel
Wm. Blair
John Reiger
James Camble
Michael Malow
John Stilt
Adam Little
John Colley

John Dunkle
Mathias Tice
Walter Cunrod
Valentine Kite
Geo. Kite
Geo. Dunkle
Thos. Barrow
Geo. Anderson
Wm. Ralston
James Bradshaw
John Davis
Andrew Full
John Bingaman
Danl. Price
John Massey
George Man
Peter Miller
Tetrarch Couch
Jacob Moyers
Stephen Hanburger
Jacob Fudge
Adam Hedrick
Nich. Mildebarler
Hy. Long
James Fowler
John Frazier
Robt. Belche
Hugh Wilson
James Lawrence
Wm. Hook
Moses Algier
Thos. Wilmouth
Adam Miller
Jacob Miller
Jacob Man
Thos. Powell
Gunrod Umble
Wm. Kinsey
Cornelius White
Nich. Null
Chas. Fie
John Early
John Ferrel
Gunrod Peterfish
Jacob Runkle
Peter Trusler
Geo. Shillinger
Arthur Trader
Nath. Harrison
Robt. Black
Matt. Black

Wm. Shannon
Thos. Pointer
Moses Samble
Hy. Coler
Jacob Richard
John Richard
Ury Umble
Danl. Cloud
Christopher Amontrout
Jacob Kindler
John Fulse
Poston Nosler
Holerick Hushman
Wm. Shaw
Martin Umble
Geo. Moffett
John Reburn
James Robertson
Alex. Craig
Saml. Kerre
John Armstrong
Adam Reburn
Robert Anderson
Edward Ervin
Fredk. Eister
Mathias Dice
John Dunkle
Ludowick Wagoner
Thos. Baskine
John Baskine
David Bell
Robt. Trimble
James Campbell
Geo. Dunkle
James Hamilton
Wm. Ervin
James Young
John Young
James Anderson
Geo. King
James Stephenson
Thos. Stephenson
John Stephenson
Gaun Leeper
Arthur Greer
Adam Miller
John Campbell
Andrew Little
Edward Ervin
Wm. Dyer

Arch. Huston
Thos. Bowne
Joseph Jenkins
Wm. Hooks
Danl. Evins
Rich. Shanklin
James Hooks
Arch. Hopkins
John Shanklin
James Fowler
John Harrison
John Gordon
Hugh McGarey
Leonard Herren
Cornelius Sullivan
Nathaniel Harrison
David Smith
Robt. McGarey
Henry Downs
Wm. Ross
Robt. McComey
Wm. Shanon
Gideon Harrison
Leonard Harring
Alex. Craig
James Alexander
Thos. Mcklemare
Thos. Spence
John Crevens
Robt. Black
Saml. Hemphill
Francis Alexander
Wm. Long
Wm. Anderson
George Robinson
Hugh Allen
Wm. Blackwood
Nathaniel Donlap
James Turk
Robt. Thomson
Anthony Black
John Black
Robt. Gibson
John Finley
John Finley, Jr.
John Patrick
James Steel
John Brown
James Allen
Saml. Henderson
James Allen, Jr.

John Young
John Vance
George Wilson
Dominick Beret
Hy. Hecks
James Lockart
Moses Thompson
John Hutcheson
James Gillaspey
Chas. Patrick
Jonathan Jones
Hugh Mackclure
Alex. Steuart
James Cull
James Bryans
Abraham Keeny
Abraham Duncklebery
Thos. Ford
Saml. Ford
James Caghey
Thos. Cashaday
Jacob Graham
John Davison
John Willey
Wm. Hambleton
Robt. Hambleton
John Gilmore
Thos. Gilmore
Jacob Cunningham
James Simpson
James Moor
Geo. Croford
Halbart McClurr
Robt. Willey
James Davis
Eldad Reed
Geo. Gipson
Robt. Tolford
David Tolford
John McAlheney
Benj. Davies
Timothy Stoten
John Putt
Joseph Clerk
John Bell
John Crockett
Danl. McBridge
James Anon
Gardner Adkins
John Hughs
John Medley

John Montgomery
Geo. Rowland
Jacob Graham
John McNeal
Henry Long
Wm. Kerr
Sampson Sayers
Saml. Bell
Wm. Hog
Wm. Eliot
Arch. Gilkson
Wm. Bell
John Trimble
John Graham
Joseph Vauhob
Robert Armstrong
Wm. Mar
John Clark
John Wilson
James Risk
George Marchel
Wm. Currey
Caleb Hermon
James Tobit
Chris. Finney
Robt. Carlile
John Williams
John Hamilton
John Matthews
John Bowen, Jr.
Henry Bowen
Moses Bowen
Reice Bowen
Geo. Matthews
John Campbell
Robt. Dew
Rich. Matthews
Michael Kelly
Danl. Goodwin
Wm. Matthews
Joshua Matthews
Wm. McKinney
Wm. Bowin
Sampson Matthews
James Wilson
James Magavock
John Armstrong
James Gilmore
Jonathan Whitley
James Hughston
Andrew Hall

Wm. Buyers
Patrick Porter
Wm. Lapesley
Arthur McClure
Saml. Todd
Robt. Brackenridge
Robt. Craig
Saml. Carr
Robt. Patterson
Thos. McCome
Geo. Moffett
Saml. Patterson
Going Leeper
James Blair
James Young
James Patterson
Alexander Craig
John Blair
John Hawl
John Thompson
Arch. Alexander
Patrick Lowry
John Lowry
Thos. Seirl
Chas. Allison
Thos. Paxton
James Huston
Robt. Henry
James Wilson
John Mayers
Geo. Davidson
Thos. Hamilton
John Plunkett
James Ward, Sr.
Wm. Ward
Joseph Ward
Alex. McMullan
Robt. Allen, Jr.
James Ward, Jr.
James Davidson
Rich. Pryar
Pat. Savage
Robt. Allen, Sr.
Phelty Cogh
Jacob Botters
Robt. Thompson
Patrick McCloskey
Edward Cenney
John Mitchel
John Tinley
Chas. McAnally

George Anderson
Wm. Polog
Geo. King
James Stewart
Arthur Greir
John King
Robt. Finley
Henry Murray
Walter Cunningham
Wm. Tencher
John Robinson
Andrew Hamilton
Wm. Anderson
Geo. Rogers
Alex. McClanahan
William Reed
Adam Dunlop
James Stephenson
Alex. Walker
John Hays
David McCroskey
John Dunlop
Andrew Buchanan
David Sayer
John Porter
David Guin
James Buchanan
James Culton
Matt. Lindsey
John Snodgrass
Wm. Buchanan
Wm. Reah
Robt. Reah
Arch. Reah
James Colter
Alex. Walker
Thos. Gilmore
John Moore
David Edmiston
John Robinson
James Berlane
Robert Stevenson
Saml. McCutchison
John Kilpatrick
Wm. Ward
John Clerk
Wm. McCutchison
James McCutchison
James Rusk
Walter Trimble
John Wilson

Robt. Hunter
Wm. Purzins
James Kenaday
Wm. Kenaday
James Wardlaw
James Logan
Saml. Huston
David Moore
Nathaniel Evans
James McClong
John McClong
Hy. McCollom
Robt. Steel
John Sproul
Moses Whiteside
John Lyle, Jr.
Robt. Lusk
John Montgomery
Arsbel Clendinin
James Steenson
James Hugart, Jr.
James McHenry
James Burnside
John Salley
Mathias Cleeke
James Steuart
David Gallaw, Jr.
Saml. McMurray
John Cantley
James Bunton
Saml. Edmiston
John Cain
John Clendinin
Andrew Buchanan
John Sprout
Thos. Vance
Wm. Matthis
John Withlaw
James Cowdown
James Steele
James Gay
Andrew Sitolentown
Dennis McNely
Lawrence Murphy
Geo. Barclay
Robt. Grimes
James Grimes
Wm. Moore
John Hudson
John McCoy
Christian Tuley

Saml. Davice
Andrew Fitzpatrick
Andrew Miscampbell
Filey Yacome
Saml. McDowell
Saml. Lyle
Patrick Lowry
John Lowry
Danl. Lyle
John Putt
Wm. Carothers
Wm. Taylor
Francis Randols
James McClung
David Bryans
David Gray
James Colter
Moses Edmiston
John McFerrin
James McFerrin
Saml. McFerrin
James Gatlive
Dennis Getty
Francis Reity
Moses Hambleton
Matt. Shaddin
John Armstrong
John Carr
Rich. Carr
Wm. Carvin
Geo. Gunn

Alex. Legat
James Stevenson
John Low
Wm. Elate
Andrew Jameson
Alex. Sutherland
Wm. Hamilton
Patrick Cargon
Thos. Smith
Ralph Laferty
James Hugart, Sr.
James Cartmill
Robt. Steuart
Geo. Jameson
John Cartmill
John Hamilton
James Milligan
Rich. Mase
Wm. McMullin
Jeremiah Green
Wm. Walker
Michael Cloyd
James Lee
James Wahreaner
Joshua McCormack
James Cloyd
David Mitchell
Bryan McDannall
David Miller
James Snodgrass

Edward Crump
John McCulley
John Stuart
Alex. McElvan
John Davis
John Hardin
John Williams
Hugh Gilespy
Hendrey McCollom
Thos. McClunge
Joseph McClunge
Robt. Montgomery
Saml. Montgomery
James Montgomery
John Montgomery
Joseph Montgomery
James Montgomery, Jr.
Thos. McFarrin
Geo. Clark
Abraham Bist
Matt. Rollin
Thos. Wilson
Abraham Thompson
James Moore
Wm. Armstrong
Dennis Gettey
Ludowick Slodser
Christopher Stoder
Saml. Rolston
Gabl. Jones
Thos. Walker

Source: Hening, Vol 7.

AMELIA COUNTY, SEPTEMBER, 1758.

Wood Jones, Major
Henry Anderson, Capt
John Winne, Capt
Branch Tanner, Lieut.

James Clark, Lieut.
Geo. Farley, Ensign
John Fitzpatrick, Ensign
Richd. Craddock, Serg.
John Cox, Serg.

Robt. Hall, Serg.
Wm. Ford, Serg.
Wm. Whitworth, Serg.
Hermon Thomas, Serg.

John Chumley
Abel Mann
John Baldwin
James Harris
John Dier
Robt. Blanchet
John Culpeper
Richd. Hoff
Wm. Forster
Francis Smith

Chas. Smith
Wm. Wood
Wm. Hudson
Christopher Hinton
Geo. Hastings
James Cheatham
Stephen Howell
Wm. Ray
John Hamton
Wm. Haynes

Robt. Fauster
Edward Farguson
John Herman
Chas. Mann
Danl. Prisnull
Thos. Wright
Ambrose Cumpton
Thos. Jones
Joel Hurt
James Hurt

Bryan Farguson
Humphrey Hendrick
Wm. Jackson
Robt. Hinton
Peter Burton
John Apling
Chas. Harrison
John Hendrick
Fredk. Reams
Saml. Mann
John Cooke
Shem Cooke
Wm. Cannon
Thos. Farguson
Peter Webster
Richd. Farguson
John Wilson
James Arnold
Wm. Childre
James Lockett
Wm. Abney
Wm. Hill
Jos. Burgess

John Hammock
John Minear
Robt. Stady
John Githings
Abram West
John James Farley
Hermon Thomson
Moses Estis
John Estis
Benj. Meadows
Wm. Person
Ralph Shelton
Wm. Harris
Robt. Hamm
Wm. Estis
John Avery
Wm. Hamm
James Campbell
Wm. Farguson
Jos. Goodman
John Brasfield
Rich. Fauster
Wm. Burgh

Wm. Hurt
John Fauster
Geo. Ridley
James Rice
Uriah Hawks
Geo. Moore
Richd. Hawks
Bell Hulm
John Moore
Thos. Hulm
Henry Clay
James Hurt, Jr.
John Loving
Wm. Hutcherson
Thos. Gunn
John Harris
Edmond Ballard
Nimrod Henson
James Hallis
Henry Paulin
Benj. Parrott
Richd. Condrow
John Harris, Jr.

Source: Hening, Vol. 7.

ALBEMARLE COUNTY, SEPTEMBER, 1758.

Jas. Nevil, Capt.
Chas. Ellis, Capt.
John Hunter, Capt.
Cornelius Thomas, Lieut.
John Freeman, Serg.

John Woods, Lieut.
Wm. Woods. Lieut.
Chas. Tuly, Ensign
Wm. Woods, Ensign
Jacob Brown, Corp.

Andrew Greer, Serg.
Chas. Wakefield, Serg.
Wm. Martin, Serg.
David Martin, Ensign
Thos. Cotrell, Corp.

Edward Weir
Thos. Powell
Malcolm Allen
Rich. Powell
Ashcroft Roach
Benj. Hensley
Wm. Henson
John Powell
Edward Spolden
Benj. Stinett
Benj. Stinett, Jr.
Henry Guffey
Wm. Williams
Solo. Carter
Joshua Fowler
John Hix
Geo. Adam Salling
John Bryan
David Davis

James Randel
Nicholas Pryor
Caleb Burton
Isham Davis
Jacob Smith
Wm. Shoemaker
Wm. Pryor
Saml. Stockton
Thos. Jameson
Hugh Alexander
Robt. Pogece
John Wallace
Adam Gaudilock
Michael Woods, Jr.
Bartholomew Ramsey
Henry Randolph
Wm. Stockton
James Kinkade
Thos. Harbet

David Gass
Abraham Howard
Thos. Grubbs
John Cowen
Geo. Brackenridge
Wm. Pogue
Wm. Wakefield
Henry Wakefield
Chas. Hughes
Aaron Hughes
Langsdon Depriest
John Depriest
James Glen
James Robertson
Chas. Crawford
John Bigs
John McAnally
Robt. McWhorter
Rich. Prior

Mark Lively
Henry Fuller
Wm. Bratchy
John Burk Lane
Stephen Cash
Philip Henson
Wm. Becknel
James White

Henry Brenton
Joshue Woods
Alex. Jameson
Danl. Maupin
John Maupin
Wm. Maupin
Matt. Mullins
Saml. Woods
Wm. Whiteside

James Martin
Michael Morrison
James Morrison
Adam Lackie
Alex. McMulen
Lawrence Smith
Matthias Hughes
Michael Israel
Wm. Cartie

Source: Hening, Vol. 7.

ACCOMAC COUNTY, SEPTEMBER, 1758.

Thomas Custis, Maj.   John Wise, Maj.

Source: Hening, Vol. 7.

BEDFORD COUNTY, SEPTEMBER, 1758.

Captains.

John Phelps
John Quarles

Matt. Talbot
Chas. Talbot

Lieutenants.

John Anthony
Wm. Irvine

Wm. Meade
Jeremiah Earley

Joseph Rentfroe
Saml. Hairston

Ensigns.

Saml. Hairston
Thos. Prateer

Thos. Gilbert
Benj. Hatcher
Jeremiah Yarborough

Robt. Hairston
Wm. Irvine

Sergeants.

John Hunter
Wm. Edwards
Ambrose Bryant
Wm. Simmons
Gross Scruggs
Meshach Haile
Rich. Andrews

Rich. Ragsdale
Rich. Callaway
Joseph Rentfroe
Thos. Prather
James Patterson
Nath. Patterson
John Hunter

Ambrose Bramlett
Wm. Bramlett
Josias Gipson
Rich. Andrews
Geo. Watts
Edmund Fair
Jacob Anderson

Jas. Callaway
John Talbot
Jas. McRonalds
Jos. Looney
Robt. Hairstone
Nicholas Hays
Thos. Cooper
Wm. Bumpass
David Rosser
Rich. Tiths
Math. Patterson
John Alston

Danl. Gilbert
Benj. Gilbert
John Hardiman
Rich. Edwards
Elliot Lacey
Chas. Harris
Geo. Caldwell
Head Lynch
Wm. Edwards
Thos. Reade
Acquiller Gilbert
Thos. Murry

Wm. Chalmor
James McRunnals
John Thompson
Abraham Mitchell
Nicholas Hays
John Pratt
Luke Murphy
James Johnston
James Patterson
John Neilson
James Morris
James Murphy

John Martin
John Lawson
Geo. Coldwell
Wm. Hinton
Jonathan Jennings
John Brown
Arch. Campbell
Francis Siver
Amhus Bramlett
Robt. Martin
Wm. Chalmore
John Spurlock
Barlet Henson
John Robertson
Wm. Manley
Wm. Twiddy
Isaac Butterworth
Joseph Ryan
Jas. McMurtry
Rich. Phillips
John Lawson
Saml. Gilbert
Danl. Gilbert
Pharoah Ryley
Wm. Fuqua
John Jackson
John Robertson, Jr.
Jacob Anderson
Patrich McDade
Christ. Sitton
John Hardman
Charles Talbot
Geo. Haynes
John Richardson
Josiah Richardson
Evan Morgan
John Morgan
John Mackey, Jr.
James Mackey
Wm. Haynes
Wm. Morgan
Thos. Morgan
Wm. Yates
Joseph Benning
John Benning
Saml. Arrenton
John Thomas
Rich. Taylor
John Moore
Zach. Robertson
Jonathan Richardson

Peter Rawlins
Peter Rawlins
Robt. Shipley
Robt. Shipley, Jr.
Anthony Rawlins
Patrick McDavid
Wm. Simmons
Zach. Burnley
John London
John Mattos
Josiah Gibson
Peter Jones
Peter Ragsdale
Geo. Abbott
Nathan Tate
Wm. Tate
Wm. Haynes
James Mackie
Robt. Oglesby
Geo. Smith
Sandiver Cashiah
Wm. Whitesite
Henry Trunk
Joseph Ray
Rich. Woodward
Thos. Pharman
Jeremiah Early
Jacob Henderson
Ambrose Bryan
Saml. Brown
James Fair
Chas. Bright
John Watts
John Handy
Matt. Talbot
Wm. Morgan, Jr.
James Board
David Preston
Evan Morgan
John Pyburn
John Wright
Geo. Grundy
Moses Trenfroe
Joseph Richardson
Edward Choat
Augustine Choat
Robt. Peper
Saml. Peper
Philip Preston
John Yates
John Robertson

Chas. Simmons
John Daunn
John Gallaway
John Dixton
Joseph Murty
Israel Young
Abraham Thompson
Wm. Bramlett
John Robinson
Wm. Nix
John Abston
Wm. Anderson
Jesse Paty
Patrick Vance
Thos. Overstreet
Wm. Stone
John Spenlock
Geo. Smith
Wm. Wooddie
Jonathan Ginnings
Wm. Ragsdale
Peter Ragsdale
Nathan Tate
Wm. Tate
Isaac Brown
John Mattocks
Peter Jones
Sandesur Keiser
Geo. Abet
Benj. Hatcher
John Mitchum
John Tinker
John Martiam
Jonathan Jones
Thos. Daws
Wm. Morgan
Wm. Board
Patrick Halloquan
John Meade
Abel Meade
James Alcorn
James Moore
John Haynes
Danl. McFall
James McFall
James Jones
Josiah Ramsey
David Irvine
Thos. Owen
Patrick Johnson
John Patrick Burks

John Grymes	Saml. Robertson	Robt. Jones
John Pyburn	Geo. Thomas	James Callaway
Thos. Hunt	Danl. Richardson	Saml. Robinson
Jeremiah Pate	Geo. Adams	Hugh Crocket
John Pate	James Moore	Thos. Baker
Matt. Pate	Jos. McDaniel	John Orrack
Anthony Pate	Nathan Richardson	John Ward
Jacob Pate	Thos. Overstreet	Jonathan Prater
John Macky	Wm. Handy	James Presnal
John Casey	Robt. Jones	Wm. Walker
John Loson	Wm. Carson	Wm. Phelps
David Loson	Stephen Rentfroe	Wm. Montgomery
Wm. Lucks	John Anderson	James Fair
Saml. Gilbert	Wm. Davis	Saml. Brown
James Bryan	Edward Davis	Rich. Woodward, Sr.
Wm. Layne	Chas. Cox	Chas. Bright
Abraham Chandler	John Riley	Edw. Bright
Jesse Bryan	Wm. Puttect	Rich. Maples
Baranabus Arthur	James Puttect	John Jones
Geo. Hackworth	James Rentfroe	Wm. Burks
Merry Carter	Nathan Pottlet	Rich. Burks
Danl. Richardson	Thos. Jones	Bolling Burks
Robt. Martin	Wm. Crabtree	Wm. Woodward
Stephen Runnals	John Davis	Rich. Woodward
Stephen Towns	James Corser	John Woodward
Barnabus Arthur, Jr.	David Morse	James Orchard
James Talbot	Reuben Keif	Edward Watts
Augustine Leftwick	Wm. Dilenham	Rich. Pritchard
John Hall	Saml. Woodward	John House
Christopher Munday	Joseph McMurty	Thos. Duly
James Millwood	Abraham McClelen	James Duly
John Snow	Thos. Oglesby	Thos. Maclin
Abraham Smith	Andrew Hairston	James Wine
James Spencer	Patrick Hensey	John Watts
Archelus McNeale	Wm. Twedey	Thos. Thirman
John Vardeman	John Gallaway	James Bromlet
Wm. Arthur	David Rosser	John Bush
Thos. Sexton	James Carson	Isaac Woodward
Moses Preston	Arch. Campbell	Michael Poore
	Edward Ohair	Andrew Poore

Source: Hening, Vol. 7.

BRUNSWICK COUNTY, SEPTEMBER, 1758.

Edward Goodrich, Capt.	Vines Collier, Ensign	Nathan Tatum, Serg.
Frederick Maclin, Lieut.	Jeptha Arthington, Ensg.	John Tilman, Serg.
John Parish, Lieut.	Thos. Briggs, Serg.	James Scott, Drummer
	Wm. Rose, Serg.	

Rich. Gower	Saml. Jackson	Nath. Steed
Wm. Parsons	Peter Freeman	Edmond Barker

Isham Harris
Wm. Bryan
James Hargrove
Robt. Wall
Chas. Wall
Peter Jackson
Frederick Glover
Thos. Mannin
Mark Jackson
Daniel Wall
Robt. Peebles
Wm. Foster
Zebulun Lewis
Jesse Brown
Wm. Parham
Nicholas Fennell
Abram Martin
Wm. Martin
John Ramsey
John Calton
Rich. Ramsey
Benj. Simpson
Thos. Connally
Thos. Haulcum
Edward Tatum
Moses Tomerlin

Edward Freeman
Henry Jackson
Chas. Gunter
John Carlile
Wm. Edwards
Elias Fowler
John Barnet
Rich. Dobbins
Joel Smith
Danl. Collier
Saml. Russell
Robt. Gee, Jr.
Wm. Cooke
Wm. Gaultney
Sampson Moseley
Geo. Walton, Jr.
Wm. Randolph
Wm. Ledbetter
Wm. Ledbetter, Jr.
Saml. Sexton
Nathan Harris
Robert Gaultney
Thos. Walton
John Moore
Robert Lanier
Thos. Denton
Wm. Denton

Lewis Barker
David Moss
James Linch
David Adam
Roger Tilman
Wm. Upchurch
Thos. Nance
Thos. Ravenscrop
Michael Upchurch
John Upchurch
Geo. Wall
Thos. Nance
John Hailes
Francis Mitchell
Tobias Moore
Robt. Nance
David Kelly
John Ray
John Tilman, Sr.
Joseph Parrish
John Woolsey
Peter Sinclair
Geo. Brewer
John Hix
Drury Sims
Mark Rollins

Source: Hening, Vol. 7.

CHESTERFIELD COUNTY, SEPTEMBER, 1758.

Robt. Kennon

Source: Hening, Vol. 7.

CUMBERLAND COUNTY, SEPTEMBER, 1758.

Robt. Slaughter, Col.
Poindexter Mosby, Capt.

Wm. Slaughter, Lieut.
Chas. Yancy, Ensign

Sergeants.

John Payton

Rich. Doggett

Hankison Read

John Parker
Wm. Lightfoot
John Ballenger
John Field
Thos. Slaughter
Francis Brown
Anthony Strother
Francis Strother
John Peyton
Wm. Baker
Wm. Edwards

John Berry
Thos. Ray
Joshua Sherril
Rueben Long
Wm. Underwood
Thos. Yeates, Jr.
John Morgan
Rich. Parker
Alex. Frazier
French Strother
Edward Bush

James Corder
John Chisum
Christopher Ziglar
Mark Hardin
Saml. Hensley
John Bradley
Rich. Parks
Allen Wiley
John Witherhead
Edward Brown
Thos. Baker

Robt. Scott	John Care	Joseph Duncan
James Browning	Wm. Thornhill	John Anderson
Henry Stronsafer	James Story	John Faver, Jr.
Wm. Wall	Wm. Poe	Wm. Collin
John Yancy	Oliver Towles	Francis Jacoby
Wm. Tutt	Saml. Pannell	Wm. Robertson
Geo. Goggins	John Banger	John Duncan
Nath. Parker	Wm. Day	Wm. Nalle, Jr.
John Shingleton	Peter Rucker	James Garrett
Chas. McQueen	Wm. Hopper	James Green
John Cox	John Pabley	Peter Fleshman
John Powell		Jacob Broil

Source: Hening, Vol. 7.

ESSEX COUNTY, SEPTEMBER, 1758.

Forest Upshaw, Capt.

Source: Hening, Vol. 7.

FREDERICK COUNTY, SEPTEMBER, 1758.

Thos. Speak, Capt.

Lieutenants.

Àrch. Ruddall	Thos. Speake	James McDowell
John Hardin		John Allen

Ensigns.

Thos. Speak	John Allen	Magnus Tatt
John Horden		James Ireson

Sergeants.

Henry Selser	James Ireson	John Champain
Chas. Littleton		Geo. Wright

John Jones	James Grigson	Robt. Stewart
Jeremiah Odle	Geo. Rice	Stephen Johnson
Moses Job	John Miller	John Regin
Reudy Mank	Wm. Jacobs	Edward Timons
Geo. Bennett	Josiah Ewings	John Colston
Jonathan Odle	Thos. Conaly	Solomon Littleton
James Thruston	Isaac Linsey	Thos. Robinson
Patrick McKenny	David James	Edward Degell
Rich. Mank	Edward Tummens	Francis McCrimer
Henry Mank	Owen Wingfield	Gasper Bewtoole
Danl. Mank	Walter Shirley	Hugh Stephenson
Henry McKenny	Jarvis Shirley	Josiah Combs
Nath. Bailey	Robt. Goosberry	James Morris
Peter Bailey	John Parke	Joseph Pierce
Wm. Cross	Isaac Thomas	Edward Mergee
Rich. Murphy	James Jack	Jacob Mergee
Danl. Johnson	Hugh Johnston	Nicholas McIntire
Stephen Southard	James Jones	Benj. Sweet
Edward Linsey	Francis Maginis	Wm. Hughs

Josiah Springer
Jacob Pricket
Stephen Stradler
Chas. Colson
John Hampton
Saml. Mason
Peter Petanger
Francis McCormack
Thos. Alfort
Rich. Stearman
Thos. Linsey
Robt. Pearis
Wm. Matthew
John Stephenson
John Vance
James Meamack
James Morris
Wm. Hall
Wm. Miller
Benj. Fullam
Wm. Locard
Levi Jones
Edward Martin
Mark Hardin
Solomon Burkem
Saml. Stubbs
Gilbert Gordon
Geo. Bell

Joseph Lyon
Thos. Allen
Andrew Blackburn
Wm. Stephenson
John Megill
Benj. Blackburn
Isaac White
Mat. Harbison
Wm. Blackburn
Bryan Money
James Hughes
Joseph Fleming
Wm. White
John Young
Joseph Taucett
John Cooper
David Williams
Leonard Cooper
Joseph Carroll
John Cook
Wm. Wilson
Saml. Vance
Andrew Vance
James Huston
Wm. Hughes
John Cooper
Danl. Johnson
Thos. Price

James Hugh
James Camp
Joseph Greenway
Wm. Wilson
Will Elimus
John Laman
James Legat
Henry Vanmeter
Jos. Vanmeter
Remembrance Williams
Edward Lucas
John Taylor
Rich. Hawkins
Joseph Wattbroke
John Vance
Ghink Doctor
John Dickson
Holloway Perry
Lawrence Landar
Joseph Polson
Wm. Frill
Robt. Buckus
Anthony Turner
John Magill
John Cook
John Duckworth
Anthony Dunlevy
Jesse Jackson

Source: Hening, Vol. 7.

FAIRFAX COUNTY, SEPTEMBER, 1758.
Captains.

Nich. Minor   James Hamilton
Josiah Clapham, Lieut.   Wm. Trammell, Ensign

Sergeants.

Chas. Martin   Jesse Martin   Francis Summers

Edward Hardin
John Donaldson
Wm. Calvin
Saml. Phillips
James Thomas
Wm. Darns
Joshua Meaks
John Wren
Wm. Shortridge
Saml. Jenkins
Saml. More
Rich. Pell
Wm. Bowling
Philip Merchant
Geo. Valendingham

Robt. Bowling
Isaac Hussey
Benj. Williams
Moses Howard
James Robinson
John Davis
Thos. Jenkins
Abraham Stiff
Joseph Adams
Joseph Bradley
Thos. Cartwright
Francis Awbrey
Joshua Claypole
Wm. O'Daniel
Thos. Saunders

Edward Rice
Wm. Cottrill
John Car
Simon Shoemaker
John Shore
Joseph Martin
Peter Wilson
Wm. Jackson
Wm. McCoy
Henry Townsend
Thos. Morgan
Thos. Ray
Wm. Massey
Franklin Perry
Geo. Shoemaker

Source: Hening, Vol. 7.

GOOCHLAND COUNTY, SEPTEMBER, 1758.

Chas. Lewis, Col,

Source: Hening, Vol. 7.

HALIFAX COUNTY, SEPTEMBER, 1758.

Abraham Maury, Col.

Captains.

Robt. Wooding	Robert Wade, Jr.	James Dillard
Peter Wilson		Thos. Callaway

Lieutenants.

Thos. Green	Thos. Spragin	Wm. Edwards
	James Dillard	

Ensigns.

Thos. Gallaway		Hugh Harris

Sergeants.

James Elkin		John Edwards

Privates.

Thos. Edwards	Rich. Moore	Wm. Murfee
Edward Peregoy	Arch. Thompson	Geo. Young
John Lewis	John Blevins	John Sillivant
Peter Manin	Clement Lee	Wm. Seales
John Childers	Wells Ward	Danl. Durbin
Wm. Simmons	Nath. Hendley	Wm. Ratcliff
Huncrest Scarlock	John Sturd	Silas Ratcliff
John Wade	James Sturd	Wm. Satterwhite
John Harris	Wm. Blevins, Jr.	John Frederick Pickle
John Rice	Josiah Cox	Danl. Newman
Thos. Norton	Ningum Prator	James Blevins
Thos. Fern	Nehemiah Prator	John Talbot
John Harris	John Blevins, Sr.	Thos. Wollin
John Rice	Wm. Asher	Pearce Gwin
Thos. Norton	John Garcer	Wm. Cox
Thos. Fern	Wm. Rickle	Wm. Blevins
John Harris, Jr.	Joseph Morton	John Williams
Benj. Croley	John Lindsey	Nath. Terry

Source: Hening, Vol. 7.

HANOVER COUNTY, SEPTEMBER, 1758.

Captains.

Christopher Hudson	Geo. Pitt

Source: Hening, Vol. 7.

HENRICO COUNTY, SEPTEMBER, 1758.

Thos. Mosely

Source: Hening, Vol. 7.

JAMES CITY COUNTY, SEPTEMBER, 1758.

Wm. Vaughan, Capt.

Source: Hening, Vol. 7.

KING GEORGE COUNTY, SEPTEMBER, 1758.

Chas. Carter, Col.
Source: Hening, Vol. 7.

Wm. Rowley, Capt.

LOUISA COUNTY, SEPTEMBER, 1758.

Saml. Waddy, Capt.

James Overton, Ensign.

Henry Dickinson	James Robinson	Thos. Jones
Clifton Rhodes	Zenus Tatt	Nick. Meriweather
Jeduthon Harper		Humphry Bickley

Source: Hening, Vol. 7.

LOUDOUN COUNTY, SEPTEMBER, 1758.

Nicholas Minor, Capt.

Aeneas Campbell, Lieut.

Francis Wilks	Wm. Stephens	John Moss, Jr.
James Willock	Robt. Thomas	John Moss
John Owsley	John Thomas	Wm. Ross

Source: Hening, Vol. 7.

LUNENBERG COUNTY, SEPTEMBER, 1758.

Wm. Caldwell, Major

Captains.

John Cargill

Pinkithman Hawkins

Lieutenants.

Cornelius Cargill, Jr.	Wm. Stokes	Thos. Boldin
Richard Dudgeon		Wm. Mitchell

Ensigns.

Wm. Hunt	James Guillum	Jacob Womack
John McNess	Thos. Jones	John Colson
	Joshua Wharton	

Sergeants.

Bryan Coker	Saml. Morton	Wm. Farrer
John Flin	Thos. Jones	Chas. Knight
Wm. Dudgeon	Peter Hamblin	John Hammons
Andrew Rogers	Jacob Gunson	Jacob Womack

Privates.

Joseph Coker	David Maddox	John Hains
John Ashworth	Thos. Jones	Thos. Pate
Isaac Ashworth	Francis Moore	James Daulton
Saml. Ashworth	John Hankins	John Lett
McKerness Good	James Fauster	Micajah Scoggins
James Bardin	Gabl. Ferriss	Rich. Jones
Wm. Blanks	John Acuff	Stephen Hatchill
Danl. Cargill	John Hall	John Pollert
Joel Elam	Thos. Smith	Wm. Parsons
James Flin	Peter Hamlin	Alex. Richey
Philip Goode	Thos. Hamlin	Wm. Harvey
	John Abraham Degranch	

John Hight
Wm. Hudson
Rich. Hudson
Francis Linsey
Henry Prewitt
Alex. Strange
John Ragsdale
Augustine Rowlands
John Thompson
Wm. Tibbs
Henry Wade
Aaron Williams
Thos. Dandy
Thos. Cargill, Jr.
Edward Darby
John Lucas
Joseph Huse
Thos. Daugherty
John McConnal
Talton East
Leonard Keeling
James Vernon
Thos. Howle
Barned Roberson
David Logan, Jr.
John East
Wm. East
Wm. Cunningham
James Ross
Robt. Sanders
John Ward
Thos. Keasy
Thos. Moore
Wm. Dickson
Thos. Pollett
John Caldwell
Robt. Caldwell
Matthew Watson
Hezekiah Jarrott
John Orr
Robt. Martin
James Caldwell
John Vernor
Rich. Berry
Rich. Adams
James Martin
Danl. Slayton
Wm. Anderson
Wm. Philby
James Doherty

Nathan Adams
David Perryman
John Perrin
Thos. Williams
John Williams
Danl. Handcock
Thos. Hall
Isaac Mundy
Rich. Hicks, Jr.
John Worsham
Wm. Skelton
Abram Martin
Wm. Poole
Geo. Levil
Edward Shipley
Abraham Vaughn
James Lett
James Worshborne
John Perrin
Nathan Adams
Thos. Smith
John Davis
James Cooper
James Norrell
Thos. Hill
Wm. Eastis
Robt. Lark
John Mannin
Aaron Drummon
Frans Atkins
Edward Atkins
Henry Stokes
Rich. Ward
Bennett Hallaway
Thos. Bell
James Spead
Wm. Ashley
Francis Norrell
John Ather
Thos. Leftwick
Merry Carter
Henry Snow
Wm. Leftwick
John Hall
Hezekiah Hall
Aquilla Hall
Jacob Matthews
Tarrence McDaniel
John Gregory
Peter Young

David Parish
Thos. McCormack
James Thweat
Nance Hitchcock
Zachariah Dode
John Mitchell
Wm. White
Edmond Hames
John Twitty Matthews
Saml. Glass
Adam Thomson
Wm. Townsend
Lawrence Matthews
Nathan Richeson
Henry Sage
Henry Talley, Jr.
John Hammons
John Coleman
Chas. Allen, Jr.
Chas. Knight
Peter Knight
Wm. Monroe
Rich. Hamblet
Saml. Wilson
James Henderson
John Bray
John McNeal
John Warren
Rich. Ragsdale
James Vaughan
Wm. Comer
Wm. Parham
Vachel Dillingham
Wm. Howard
Ephraim Hudson
James Kidd
Nathan Ellis
James Ellis
Reuben Keith
Wm. Dillingham
Geo. Benn
Arthur Matthews
John Worsham
John Hankins
John Hall
Robt. Hall
Wm. Russell
Francis Moore
Abraham Womack
John Mitchell

Source: Hening, Vol. 7.

MIDDLESEX COUNTY, SEPTEMBER, 1758.

Christopher Curtis, Capt.
Source: Hening, Vol. 7.

NANSEMOND COUNTY, SEPTEMBER, 1758.

Edward Wright, Capt.
Source: Hening, Vol. 7.

NORTHAMPTON COUNTY, SEPTEMBER, 1758.

John Haggoman, Capt.   Michael Dixon   John Pigot
Source: Hening, Vol. 7.

NORTHUMBERLAND COUNTY, SEPTEMBER, 1758.

William Taite, Maj.   John Heath
Source: Hening, Vol. 7.

NEW KENT COUNTY, SEPTEMBER, 1758.

Chas. Crump, Capt.   Thos. Morton
Source: Hening, Vol. 7.

PRINCESS-ANNE COUNTY, SEPTEMBER, 1758.

Christopher Wright, Capt.
Source: Hening, Vol. 7.

PRINCE EDWARD COUNTY, SEPTEMBER, 1758.

Philemon Halcomb, Capt.   John Nash, Jr., Capt.   Henry Watkins, Ensign
Source: Hening, Vol. 7.

PRINCE GEORGE COUNTY, SEPTEMBER, 1758.

Richard Bland, Col.   Richard Bland, Jr., Capt.
Source: Hening, Vol. 7.

PRINCE WILLIAM COUNTY, SEPTEMBER, 1758.

Henry Lee, Col.

Captains.

Wm. Tebbs   Thos. McClanaham
                    John Markham, Corp.
Source: Hening, Vol. 7.

SURRY COUNTY, SEPTEMBER, 1758.

Wm. Seward, Jr., Capt.
Source: Hening, Vol. 7.

SUSSEX COUNTY, SEPTEMBER, 1758.

James Wyche, Capt.
Source: Hening, Vol. 7.

SOUTHAMPTON COUNTY, SEPTEMBER, 1758.

Peter Butts, Capt.
Source: Hening, Vol. 7.

SPOTSYLVANIA COUNTY, SEPTEMBER, 1758

Thos. Estis, Capt.
Source: Hening, Vol. 7.

STAFFORD COUNTY, SEPTEMBER, 1758.

Withers Conway, Capt.

Source: Hening, Vol. 7.

WESTMORELAND COUNTY, SEPTEMBER, 1758.

John Martin, Maj.   John Newton, Capt.

Source: Hening, Vol. 7.

YORK COUNTY, SEPTEMBER, 1758.

John Prentis, Maj.   Robt. Shield, Capt.

Source: Hening, Vol. 7.

AUGUSTA COUNTY, 1763.

Andrew Lewis, Col.	Wm. Preston, Maj.	Benj. Harrison, Capt.
Robt. Brackenridge	Michael Terbolt	John Smith
Edward Carwin	John Armstrong	Saml. Meredith
James Hughes	Lantey Armstrong	Robt. Kirkum
John Crawford	John Donnelly	Joseph Bates
	James Bryan	

Source: Hening, Vol. 8.

AUGUSTA COUNTY, 1759.

Captains.

John Smith		Alex. Sayers (decd.)
Audley Hall, Lieut.		Joseph Ray, Sergt.
Robert Steel	Abram Thomson	Chas. Lockart
James Haynes	James Stewart	Saml. Vance
Chas. Ramsey	James Berry	Alex. Collier
John Greenlee	James Amox	John Cox
James Greenlee	James Dooley	David Cox
Chas. Slinker	Henry Dooley	James Arbuckle
Saml. Newbery	Abraham Dooley	Matt. Arbuckle
Wm. McDonald	Danl. Young	John Arbuckle
John Robertson	Edmund Young	Gilbert Christian
Henry Filbrick	Thos. Caldwell	John Gregory
Joseph McClellan	Humphrey Baker	Arthur Campbell
	James Hay	

Source: Hening, Vol. 8.

ALBEMARLE COUNTY, 1756.

Wm. Fuqua   Thomas Walker

Source: Hening, Vol. 8.

BEDFORD COUNTY, 1758.

Wm. Irvine

Source: Hening, Vol. 8.

CHESTERFIELD COUNTY, 1760.

Abel Farrar, Lieut.   Stephen Blankenship

Source: Hening, Vol. 8.

FREDERICK COUNTY, 1759.

Luke Collins, Capt.   Rich. Pearis
Source: Hening, Vol. 8.

HALIFAX COUNTY, 1759.

Joshua Powell
Source: Hening, Vol. 8.

HALIFAX COUNTY, 1760.

Geo. Boyd, Lieut.
Source: Hening. Vol. 8.

HALIFAX COUNTY, 1763.

Robt. Wade, Capt.   Peter Rogers, Lieut.   James Lyon, Ensign
John Link, Sergt.   Henry Strugs, Sergt.

John Dean	John Login	James Page
Stephen Terry	Thos. Hicks	Bryan Nowling
Rich. Murfey	Wm. Falling	Frederick Edwards
Joshua Jones	John Hampton	Edward Morgan
Jonathan Jones	Rich. Griffin, Jr.	Jacob Bouyiis
John Bently	John Smith	Wm. Robinson
Wm. Follas	James Symms	Wm. Rosebury
Wm. Bell	Abram Whitter	John Ray
Rich. Condron	Elisha Pierce	Joshua Smith
John Dyer	Edward Cason	John Goff
Elias Brock	Larkin Cason	Frederick Farmer
Jacob Shepard	John Jennings	David Hamby
David Bolling	John Salmon	Jonathan Hamby
Berton Link		Rich. Turner

Source: Hening, Vol. 8.

KING AND QUEEN COUNTY, 1757.

John Richards
Source: Hening, Vol. 8.

LOUDOUN COUNTY, 1757.

Stephen Thatcher   Thomas Bond
Source: Hening, Vol. 8.

LOUDOUN COUNTY, 1763.

Capt. Moss   Lieut. Gore
Source: Hening, Vol. 8.

LUNENBURG COUNTY, 1758.

Bryan Lester
Source: Hening, Vol. 8.

NORFOLK COUNTY, 1758.

Henry Darnell
Source: Hening, Vol. 8.

PRINCE WILLIAM COUNTY, 1763.

Wm. Baylis
Source: Hening, Vol. 8.

Lord Dunmore's War, 1774.

Muster rolls of companies defending the frontier.
A list of Captain Daniel Smith's Company of Fincastle Militia.

Daniel Smith, Captain
William Bowen, Lieut.

John Kinckeid, Ensign
David Ward, Ensign

Privates.

Drury Pricket (Pucket)	James Kendrick	Burton Litton
Joseph Horne	Thomas Mullin	Benj. Jones
James Scott	Alden Williams	Robert Griffin
James Price	Charles ——	Thomas Price
Saml. Dollarhide	Robert Brown	Richard Price
Christian Bergman	James Smith	Wm. McFarland
David Kingkeid, Jr.	Archelaus Scott	John Courtney
William Neale	Joseph Olverson	
Robert Donalson	Samuel Vanhook	

Source: Draper MSS. (Undated List, 4XX61).

List of men contd. in a letter of Michael Woods to Col. William Preston.

Joseph Inglish	Robert Wiley, Snr.	Wm. Cavanough, Snr.
William Cliften	Thomas Wiley	John Umphres
James Williams	Samuel Astle	John Nicklas
Henry Walker	William Lesey	George Sobe
Richard Woods	Jeremiah Cary	Peter Dingos
Charles Atkins	Joshua Inglish	Robert Wiley, Jnr.
Samuel Camble	Andrew Woods	Thomas Haket
Squire Gatleph	Adam Clendenin	Ishmall Babit
Richard Herd	Adam Woods	Henry Oharron
George Scott	Henry Atkins	
Francis Rowan	Michael Woods	

Source: Draper MSS. (3QQ30).

List of men contd. in a letter from Thomas Burk to Col. Preston. May ye 30, 1774.

Henry Librough	Philip Martin	William Lucas
Edward Hale	George Martin, Jnr.	Christy Martin
John Lucas	George Fry, Jnr.	Willinton Adkins
Charles Lucas, Jnr.	Thomas Hale	

Source: Draper MSS. (3QQ31).

A list of Robert Doack's Company of Militia, June 2, 1774.

John Stephens, Lieut.		William Meek, Serjeant
Andrew Thompson, Ensign		William Doack, Ensign
William Ward, Serjeant		James Downy, Serjeant
David Doack, Jnr.	John Pierce	Samuel Ewing

John Stephens
Adam Walker
Samuel Doack
John Williams
John Nowell
Jacob Kinder
Andrew Bronstetter
Thomas Bell
Moses Moor
John Gilihan
Martin Staily
Christly Weaver
John Bunshell
Henry Waggoner
Michael Grigger
Nicholas Cloyne
Patrick Johnston
Charles Fullen
Duncan Gullion
Jacob Kinsor
Michael Kinsor
John King
William Campbell
Bezaleel Maxwell
David Maxwell
John Henderson
Francis Catron
John Downy
Thomas Mead
Arnold Shell
Moses Gordon
Samuel Moor
George Kinder
Hugh Robinson
Peter Kinder
Jacob Dobler
Samuel Handly

Michael Weaver
John Messersmith
Barnet Messersmith
Henry Waggoner, Jnr.
Peter Grigger
Campbell Baily
Barny Gullion
John Gullion
Jacob Catron
Walter Kinsor
William King
Samuel Campbell
John Maxwell
Robert Stephenson
William Litz
Frederick Rap
Jacob Catron
Adam Catron
Philip Catron
Peter Hedrick
John Cattes
George Wambler
Frederick Moor
Jacob Hamilton
Thomas Hamilton
George Carr
William Carr
Roger Cats
John Crawford
John Irvine
William Litz
James Douglass
Thomas Rodgers
John Lesly
George Vaut
James Mitchell
Philip Dutton

Alexander Ewing, Jr.
Archibald Reagh
Samuel Paxton
Robert Miller
George Henly
Andrew Vaut
Jacob Blesly
John Adams
Peter Catron
Michael Staffy
Michael Walter
Mitchael Wambler
Adam Boh
Isaiah Hamilton
Francis Hamilton
Michael Catron
James Carr
Ben Rutherford
John Vails
John Diver
Robert Stephenson
George Douglass
James Rodgers
Daniel Henderson
Samuel Henderson
Thomas Mitchell
John Nuland
Alexander Ewing
William Ewing
John Reagh
Paddy Saint Lorrance
Robert Porter
William Henly
Christly Vaut
John Carr
John Blesly

Source: Draper MSS. (3QQ34).

Fragment of Muster Roll of Capt. Wm. Campbell's Company.   July, 1774.

Philemon Higgins
Joseph Newberry
Stephen Hopton
John Lewis
William Hopton

John Neil
Richard Lyhnam
John Boles
Benjamin Richardson
John Johnston

Richard Woolsey
Audlin Williamson
Conrad Sterns
William Richardson
William Champ

Source: Draper MSS. (3QQ63).

A list of men in Capt. Daniel Smith's Company, 13 Aug., 1774.
The following list of garrisons in the border forts is found in two documents, which have been combined into one.   "E. G." indicates Elk Garden; "M. S.," Maiden Spring; "W.," Whitton's Crab Orchard Fort.   The first five men on the list were discharged Nov. 18th, after ninety-eight days' service.

At the Elk Garden Fort.

Robert Brown, Sergeant, found bread 15 days, M. S. till 23d, then W.
John Lewis, listed 13th Aug. E. G.
Ericus Smith, E. G.　Found bread till 29th Aug.
James Laughlin, E. G.　"　"　"　"　"
William Priest, E. G.　"　"　"　"　"
Robert Breeze, E. G.　"　"　"　"　"
Benjamin Jones, E. G.　Discharged 29th Aug.
Samuel Priest, E. G.　Discharged 29th Aug.　He found bread.
Thomas Jones, W.　He found bread.　Listed 14th; discharged 29th.
Thomas Price, E. G.　Found bread.
Thomas Donelson, E. G.　Found bread.
Robert Donelson, E. G.　Found bread.
Richard Breeze, W.　Listed 17th; discharged 29th.
Thomas Brumly, M. S.
James Rogers, M. S.　Listed 22nd; discharged 29th.
David Priest, E. G.　Found bread.
Henry Manadue, E. G.　Found bread.
James Anderson, E. G.　Listed 23d; discharged 29th.　Found bread.
Richard Price, E. G.　Listed 23rd; discharged 29th.　Found bread.
John Kingkeid, E. G.　Listed 14th Aug.　Found bread.
David Kingkeid, E. G.　Listed 14th Aug.　Found bread.

The 29th Aug. all the above men except the first five were discharged.
Mr. John Kingkeid was then appointed their Sergeant the 12th Sept.　He
took into pay:

James Anderson	Henry Manadue	Richard Price
Ben Jones	Robert Brown, 2d Sept.	David Kingkeid
David Priest	Robert Donelson	Thomas Donelson
Samuel Priest	Thomas Price	

At the Glade Hollow Fort.

Ensign Hendly Moore
Mr. John Dunkin, Sergeant
James McCarty ⎫
Archibald Scott ⎪
James Price ⎬ Listed 29th Aug.
Drury Pricket ⎪
Jeremiah Able ⎭
James Scott ⎫
Isaac Crisman ⎪
William Ferrill ⎬ Listed 19th Sept.
Richard Thompson ⎪
Francis Cooper ⎭
William Pharis, 29th Aug., discharged 25th Oct.　W.
Solomon Litton
James Coyle ⎫
William Wilmoth ⎬ 29th Sept.
Joseph Horn ⎭
Richard Byrd

Abraham Cooper, Oct. 29–Nov. 18.
Archibald Woods, Oct. 31–Nov. 18.
William Bustar, Nov. 6–Nov. 18.

> Editor's Note.—The last three names are found in the second list only. They apparently enlisted after returning from the Point Pleasant expedition.

At the Maiden Springs Station, 26th Aug., 1774.

Mr. Robert Brown, Sergeant till 23rd Sept., then Joseph Cravens.
Henry Willis.
Joseph Cravens.
James M'Clehany, discharged 19th Oct. 55 days.
James Cravens.
John Jameson, listed 29th Aug.; discharged 19th Oct. 53 days.
James Rogers.
Thomas Brumly, listed 22nd Aug.; discharged 19th Oct. 60 days.
Andw. Lammy, listed 16th Aug.; 4th Sept. Saml. Fowler came in his room.
John Flintham, listed 14th Aug.; discharged 19th Oct. 68 days.
James Douglas, M. S.
John Newland, W. ⎫
Samuel Paxton, W. ⎬ Listed Sept. 14th, discharged 22nd. 8 days.
Philip Dutton, W. ⎭
John Cravens, M. S., 23rd Sept.
Rees Bowen, Aug. 26–Sept. 2.
David Ward, Aug. 26–Sept. 2.
Robert Cravens, Nov. 1st–Nov. 18th.

At the Upper Station.

Mr. John Campbell, Ensign.
Isaac Spratt, Sergeant, listed 15th Aug.
George Dohorty, listed 15th Aug.; 25th Sept. went away without leave.
Andrew Steel, listed 15th Aug.; Oct. 18th discharged. 64 days.
John Hambleton, listed 15th Aug.; discharged 18th Oct. 64 days.
Alexander Grant, listed 15th Aug.; deserted 8th Sept.
David Bustar, listed 29th Aug.
William Thompson, listed 29th Aug.
Edward Sharp, 7th Sept. listed; discharged 21st. 14 days.
Michael Glaves, 6th Sept. Went away without leave 7th Oct.
James Fullen, 5th Sept.; discharged 21st. 16 days.
James Edwards, 5th Sept. Went away without leave 30th Sept.
John Williams, 7th Sept.; discharged 16th. 9 days.
Thomas Potter, 5th Sept. Went away without leave 7th Oct. Came back.
Levi Bishop, 8th Sept.; 22nd Sept.
Robert Moffet, 8th Sept.
Alexander Henderson, 15th Sept. Went away 12th Oct.
Francis Hambleton, 15th Sept. Went out without leave 25th Sept. Came back.
John Crafford, 15th Sept.; discharged 24th. 10 days.
Isaiah Hambleton, 15th Sept.; 22nd Sept. went away without leave.
Benjamin Rediford, 15th Sept.; 26th, went away, came back Oct. 1st.
Andrew Branstead, 15th Sept.; 26th, went away, came back Oct. 1st.

James Mitchell, 15th Sept.; 26th, went away, came back Oct. 1st.
Rowland Williams, 15th Sept.
Mr. Thomas Whitten, Senr., appointed Sergeant 26th Sept.
Thomas Whitten, Jnr., Oct. 1st.
John Grinup, Oct. 1st.
Francis Hynes, Oct. 1st.
Samuel Doack, listed Oct. 1st, went away 12th Oct.
Thos. Rogers, listed Oct. 1st, went away 12th Oct.
John Lashly, listed Oct. 1st, went away 12th Oct.
William King, Oct. 1st
Thos. Meads, Oct. 1st.
Jacob Kindar, Oct. 1st.
Daniel Henderson, Oct. 10th.
Peter Kindar, Oct. 10th.
Jonathan Edwards, in his brother's room, 6th Oct.
Christian Bergman, 5th Oct.
Michael Razor, 24th Oct.
Jeremiah Whitton, 27th Oct.

Scouts.

William Bowan, Aug. 12th.
James Fowler.
Thomas Maxwell, 10 days.   June 11th.
Rees Bowan.
David Ward.
John Kingkeid, 17 days.
William Priest, 7 days.
John Sharp, 10 days.
William Crabtree.
Samuel Hays.
Robert Davis, 15 days of his time to go to Robt. Moffet.
At Elk Garden, 1 Sergeant, 15 men.
Fort Christian, 1 Ensign, 1 Sergeant, 15 men.
Maiden Springs, Brown and Cravens and 12 men.
Whittons, 1 Ensign, Spratt and Whitten and 44 men.

Source: Draper MSS. (5XX2; 6XX106).

A list of Capt. William Nalle's Company of Volunteers from Augusta County.

September, 10th day, 1774.

William Nalle, Captain   William Bush, Sergeant
Jacob Pence, Ensign   Barnod Crafford, Sergeant
Martain Nalle, Lieut.   John Bush, Sergeant

William Feavil	Henry Miner	James Washbun
Moses Smith	Sefniah Lee	James Alexander
Israel Meader	Mecagh Smith	Joseph Roay
John Grigsby	John Deek	John Pright
Zacarias Lee	John Williams	John Owler
Benjamin Petty	James Selby	James Miller
Bruten Smith	Abraham Rue	John Chism
William Spicer	John Null	Henry Cook
Charles Brown	Shadrick Butler	Thomas Brook (Confined)

George Rucker
William Scails
Yenty Jackson
George Fuls
George Harmon
Adam Hansburger
John Breden

Robert Rains
Steven Washburn
Henry Owler
Richard Welsh
John Goodall
Michael Gurden
James Todd

Chesly Rogers
Zacarias Plunkepel
William Smith
John Fry
Joseph Butler
James Reary
Jacob Null

Source: Draper MSS. (2ZZ30).

A list of John Murray's Company of Volunteers from Botetourt.
September 10th, 1774.

John Murray, Captain
Samuel Wallace, Lieut.
William Taylor, Sergeant
John Larken, Sergeant
Barney Boyls, Sergeant

Wm. McKee, Lieut.
Adam Wallace, Ensign
Moses Coiler, Sergeant
John Simpson, Sergeant

Hugh Logan
James Arnold
Stephen Arnold
William Moor
John Nelson
John Sedberry
William McCorkle
George Milwood
Andrew Evins
Joseph McBride
Thomas Nail
John Lapsly
James Walker
Ezekiel Kennedy
John Jones
John Moor
William Simpson
Thomas McClure
John McClure
Peter Kasheday
Robert Wallace
Thomas Peary
John Grigs

George Cummins
John Eager
Hugh Logan
James Neely
Peter Higans
William Bradly
William Brown
John Barkly
Isaac Trimble
William Johns
James Bambrige
John Gilmor
James Hall
James Crawley
Daniel Blair
Thomas Burny
Daniel Simkins
William Lyons
James Simkins
Nicholas Mooney
Solomon Brundige
Stephen Harris
Daniel Fullin

David Wallace
Moses Whitby
James Gilmor
James Cunningham
John Kelsey
Hugh Moor
Joseph Gibson
William Cochran
James Logan
John Logan
Thomas Hedden
Prisley Gill
John Coiler
Johnathan Watson
William Neely
John Milican
William Connor
John McGee
James McCalister
Andrew Wallace
Peter McNeil
Andrew Alden
John Murray

Source: Draper MSS. (2ZZ32,33).

A Roll of Capt. Philip Love's Company of Volunteers.
There are two lists of the company of Capt. Philip Love. The second, dated Oct. 7th, contains but one additional name—James Neeley, Cadet.
Sept. 10th, 1774.

Phi. Love, Capt.
John Mills, Ensign
Francis McElhaney, Quarter M. S.
James Alexander, Sergeant

Daniel McNiell, Lieut.
Wm. Ewing, Sergt. Major
Sieltor Taylor, Sergeant
John Craford, Sergeant

Robert Owen
Sam. Andrews
William Scott

Thomas Welch
Thos. Welch, Jnr.
Patrick Conner

John Buchanan
Charles Davis, Batman
Wm. Franklin

Sam. Mt. Gumry Joseph Pain James Franklin
  (Montgomery) Will Armstrong Wm. Hanson
William Teasy Daniel McDonald James McDonald
John Dodd James Simson Richard Collins
Thos. Perce Thomas Brown James M. Guillin
Thos. Armstrong James Neeley John McGinness
John Dunn Abraham Moon, Batman Griffin Harriss
Charles Byrne to Colo. Lewis John Jones, Cadet
Thomas Gilberts George Craig, Batman to John Markes
Abraham Demonse Colo. Lewis John Robinson, Batman
Will Hooper Richd. Willson, Carpenter John Todd, Cadet
Sam Savage Robt. Smith, Batman Daniel Ormsbey, Batman

Source: Draper MSS. (2ZZ32,33).

A list of Capt. John Lewis' Company of Volunteers from Botetourt.

The Draper MSS. contains two lists of this company. The difference is in the last seven names, which have been transferred from the second list, while the alternative spelling of names is derived from the same source.

John Henderson, Lieut. Robert Alliet (Eliott) Ins.
Samuel Glass, Sergeant William Bryans, Sergeant
Peter Huff, Sergeant William Wilson, Sergeant
Samuel Estil, Sergeant John Donally, Fife
Thomas Alsbury, Drum

Privates.

John Swoop Peter Hendrix Isaac Nickels
Alexander Kelley John Hundley Philip Hammon
Edward Egins Thomas Huff James Burtchfield
James Ellison Thomas Edger Solomon White
John Deniston Molastin Peregin Thomas Carpender
James Stuart James McNitt Solomon Carpender
John Savage Nathan Farmer Jeremiah Carpender
Christopher Welsh John Carpender David Cook
James Crawley (Croley) Adam Caperton John Boughman
James Dulin Mathew Creed Jacob Boughman
Isaac Fisher James Charlton Robert Bowles
Peter Ellenburgh Mathew Polug James Burnsides
Andrew Kissinger Thomas Kanady (Canady) Dennis Nail
Samuel Barton William Jones Henry Howard
William Clifton Richard Packwood Walter Holwell
Joseph Love John Arthur Samuel Burcks
Leonard Huff William Robison Gabriel Smithers
Samuel Croley Samuel Huff Thomas Burnes
William Isum Edward Wilson Hugh Caperton
Isaac Taylor Robert Boyd
Martin Carney John Reburn

2nd List.

Matt. Jewitt William Man Mathias Kisinger
William Boniface Adman Cornwell
Henry Boyer Robert Davis

Source: Draper MSS. (2ZZ27, 28).

A list of Capt. Buford's Company of Volunteers from Bedford Co.

Thomas Dooley, Lieut.
Nicholas Mead, Sergeant
John Fields, Sergeant
Abraham Sharp on Comd.

Jonathan Cundiff, Ensign
Wm. Kenedy, Sergeant
Thomas Fliping, Sergeant
Absalom McClanahan on Comd.

William Bryant
Wm. McColister
James Scarbara
John McClanahan
James McBride
John Carter
William Overstreet
Robert Hill
Samuel Davis
Zachariah Kennot
Augustine Hackworth
William Cook
Uriah Squires
Thomas Hall

William Hamrick
Nathaniel Cooper
John Cook
Mr. Waugh, cadet
John McGlahlen
John Campbell
William Campbell
Adam Lin
Thomas Stephens
William Keer
Gerrott Kelley
James Ard
William Deal
John Bozel
John Welch

Thomas Hamrick
James Boyd
James Dale
Robert Ewing
Francis Seed
William Hackworth
John Roberts
Joseph White
Joseph Bunch
Jacob Dooley
Thomas Owen
John Read
John Wood, cow driving
Robert Boyd

Source: Draper MSS. (2ZZ36).

Captain Stewart's Company.   (From torn MS. in his own writing).

Charles O'Haara, Sergeant
Skidr. Harriman, Sergeant

James Donaley, Sergeant

Daniel Workman
Samuel Williams
Wm. O'Harra
Robert O'Harra
James Paulley
James Clarke
John Pauley
Arch. McDowell
Wm. Hogan
Andrew Gardner
Qeavy Lockhart

Samuel Sullivan
Thomas Fargison
John McCandless
Thomas Gillespy
Henry Lawrance
John Crain
William Dyer
Edward Smith
John Harris
Joseph Current
Wm. Clindinning

Spencer Cooper
Daniel Taylor
Joseph Day, on Comd.
Jacob Lockhart, on Comd.
George Clinding
John Burke
Charles Keeneson
William Ewing
John Doherty
John McNeal
Joseph Campbell

Source: Draper MSS. (2ZZ40).

A list of Capt. Robert McClenachan's Company of Volunteers from Botetourt.

William McCoy, Lieut.
Thomas Williams, Sergeant
Samuel Clark, Sergeant

Matthew Bracken, Ensign
William Craig, Sergeant
William Jones, Drum

John Harmon
James Kinkaid
George Kinkaid
David Cutlip
James Morrow, Senr.
James Morrow
James Gilkeson
Even Evens
William Stewart

Edward Thomas
Patrick Constantine
William Custer
Lewis Homes
William Hutchisen
Edward Barret
John Williams
Richard Williams
James Burrens

John Patten
Thomas Ellias
Charles Howard
James Guffy
Thomas Cooper
William McCaslen
John Cunningham
Francis Boogs
John Vaun

Source: Draper MSS. (2ZZ39.)

Capt. Pauling's list of Botetourt troops.

Henry Pauling, Capt.		Edward Gouldman, Lieut.
Samuel Baker, Ensign		Obediah H. Treat, Sergeant
Robert Findley, Sergeant		James Woods, Sergeant
Robert Watkins	Thomas Wilson	John Aggnue
Philip Hanee	Alexr. Culwell on Comd.	James Donoho
James Dehority	William Gilliss	Thomas Reid
William Thompson	Edward Ross	Joseph Whitticor
William Holley	Matthew Ratliff	Isham Fienquay, canoe
Joel Doss	William Glass	David Condon, canoe
William Ray	John Fitzhugh	Richard Lemaster
Dangerfield Harmon	William Canaday	James King
Stephen Holston	John Clerk	John Hutson
James Wilson	John Frazer	William Macalister
Dudley Callaway, canoe	George Davis	Jeremiah Jenkins
David Bellew, canoe	Thomas Mecrary	Edward Carther
Andrew Rodgers	Richd. Rollens	Martin Baker
Robert Ferrill	Mical Luney	James Lyn
Andrew Harrison	John Gibson	
George Simmerman	Charles Ellison	

Source: Draper MSS. (2ZZ41).

A list of Capt. Evan Shelby's Company of Volunteers from Fincastle.
The original list is in Capt. Evan Shelby's own handwriting. The names of the officers as far as known were, Isaac Shelby, Lieut.; James Robertson and Valentine Sevier, Sergeants.

1 Capt.	George Ruddle	Richard Burck
1 Lieut.	Emanuel Shoatt	John Riley
1 Ensign	Abram Bogard	Elijah Robison
4 Sergeants	Peter Torney	Rees Price
4 Canoe Men	William Tucker	Richard Holliway
1 on Com.	John Fain	Jarrett Williams
James Shelby	Saml. Vance	Julias Robison
John Sayers	Saml. Fain	Charles Fielder
John Findley	Saml. Hensley	Benj. Grayum
Henry Shaw	Saml. Samples	Andrew Goff
Daniel Mungle	Arthur Blackburn	Hugh Ogullion
John Williams	Robert Herrill	Barnett Ogullion
John Carmack	Geo. Armstrong	Patrick St. Lawrence
Andrew Terrence	William Casey	Jos. Hughey
George Brooks	Mark Williams	John Bradley
Isaac Newland	John Stewart (wounded)	Basilael Maxwell
Abraham Newland	Conrad Nave	

E. SHELBY.

Total, 45 privates, including six of Captain Herbert's men from Fincastle.
7 Octr., 1774.

Source: Draper MSS. (2ZZ37, 38).

Return of troops camped at Point Pleasant under command of Colonel Willam Fleming.

List of Wounded Men now on my List.   Octr. 23, 1774.

Capt. Shelby's Company.
  John Stuart
  Reece Price
  John Cormick
Capt. Russell's Company.
  John Basdel
  William Prince
Capt. Campbell's Company.
  Thomas Baker
Capt. Arbuckle's Company.
  John McMullin
  David Glascum
  John Freeland
  William Morris

Capt. Lewis's Company.
  Thos. Hoof (Huff)
  Thomas Carpenter
Capt. Love's Company.
  James Alexander
  William Franklin
Capt. McKee's Company.
  Stephen Arnold
Capt. Stuart's Company.
  Charles Kinson
  Thomas Fourgeson
Major Robertson's Company.
  Henry Bowyer
Capt. Herbert's Company.
  James Newell

Source: Draper MSS. (2ZZ35).

Capt. James Harrod's Party, 1774.

The men in the following list were the pioneers of Harrod's Kentucky settlement. Twenty-two of their number enlisted under Harrod and joined Col. Christian's division of Fincastle troops that arrived at Point Pleasant after the battle.

James Harrod
Azariah Davis
Arthur Campbell
William Campbell
John Cowan
William Fields
William Martin
David Williams
James Kerr
Silas Harlan
Joseph Blackford

Patrick Doran
James Sanders
Davis Glenn
James Wiley
John Shelp
James Davis
Elijah Harlan
William Crow
William Myres
Jared Cowan
John Crow

Abraham Chapline
Henry Hogan
John Smith
James Brown
Azariah Reese
Martin Stull
William Garrett
John Clark
William Venable

Source: Draper MSS. from the McAfee Papers. (14J, 128).

PARTIAL LIST OF THE OFFICERS KILLED AND WOUNDED AT THE BATTLE OF POINT PLEASANT, OCT. 10, 1774.

Field Officers Killed.

Col. Charles Lewis   Col. Jno. Field.

Field Officers Wounded.

Col. Wm. Fleming.

Captains Killed.

John Murray   Robt. McClenahan
Saml. Wilson   Charles Ward

Captains Wounded.

Thos. Buford   John Skidmore
John Dickison

Subalterns Killed.

Lieut. Hugh Allen   Ensign Cundiff
Ensign Matt. Brakin

Subalterns Wounded.

Lieut. Lard   Lieut. Golman
Lieut. Vance   Lieut. James Robison

Source: Niles Weekly Register, Vol, 12, p. 145.

PARTIAL LIST OF OFFICERS AND MEN AT THE BATTLE OF POINT PLEASANT, Oct. 10, 1774. (K—Killed).

Andrew Lewis, Brig.-General, Commanding.

Colonels.

Charles Lewis (K)	Wm. Christian
William Fleming	John Field (K)

Captains.

Matt. Arbuckle	—— Love	James Robertson
Thos. Buford	Wm. McKee	Wm. Russell
Jno. Draper	Robert McClanahan (K)	John Stewart
John Dickinson	Saml. McDowell	Evan Shelby
James Harrod	Wm. Christian	Wm. Shelby
—— Herbert	John Field (K)	—— Slaughter
Joseph Haynes	Alex. McClanahan	I. Skidmore
Benj. Harrison	Geo. Matthews	Dan'l. Smith
John Lewis	John Murray (K)	James Ward
John Lewis 2nd	Wm. Paul	Sam'l Wilson
—— Lockridge	—— Paulin	

Lieutenants.

Hugh Allen (K)	Thos. Ingles	—— Tate
John Draper	—— Lard	——Vance
—— Goldman	—— Robinson	
John Henderson	Isaac Shelby	

Ensigns.

Bracken (K)	—— Cantiff (K)

Privates.

Wm. Arbuckle	Simon Gerty	—— Robinson
Jno. Arbuckle	Ellis Hughes	Alex. Reed
—— Blair	Philip Hammond	Jno. Steele
—— Clay (K)	—— Hickman (K)	—— Trotter
—— Coward	Saml. Lewis	James Trimble
Wm. Campbell	Thomas Lewis	John Van Bibber
Jno. Campbell	Simon Kenton	Peter Van Bibber

Chas. Clendenin   Sam'l McCullock   James Welch
Robert Clendenin   Wm. Moore   Bazatell Wells
Leonard Cooper   Walter Newman
Wm. Eastham   John Pryor

Commissary-General.

Thomas Posey

Butcher.

Jacob Warrick

Sutler.

John Frog (K)

Source: West Va. Hist. Mag., Vol. 2, p. 30.

Augusta County Militia in 1742.

Company No. 1.

James Patton, Col.
John Smith, Capt.
John Moffit, Lieut.

Will Anderson, Ensign
Dan Danniston, Serj.

Sam. Hogshead
John Hogshead
Will Hogshead
Dan McAnear
Math. Edmestan
John Finley
Walter Trimble
John Francis
Rob Ralston
John Young
Alex. Blair
Alex. Craig
Thos. Gillespy
And. Erwing
Benj. Erwine
John Erwine
Edw. Erwine

John Trimble
Jas. Trimble
Rob. Moffet
Jas. Wright
John Anderson
Rob. King
Rob. Poage
Jas. Armstrong
Rob. Patterson
John Pattison
Jas. Craford
Jas. Lesley
Will Barkins
Felix Kanady
Thos. Gordon
And. Mitchel
Jas. Robertson

Gabl. Pickins
Rob. Leeper
Sam. Moore
John Miller
Jas. Miller
Patr. Quine
Mat. Armstrong
John Ramsey
Dan. Danniston
Sam. Northward
Rob. Renick
John Archer
Sampson Archer
James Sayers
Thos. McCulough
Geo. Anderson

Company No. 2.

John Buchanan, Capt.
Will Evins, Lieut.

Jos. Cotton, Ensign
John Mitchel, Serj.

Joseph Kanada
Jams. Cooke
Chas. Donooho
Solo. Moffot
Jas. Sunderlin
Will. Sayers
John Dyche
Rob. Cotton
Chas. Camble
Sam. Walker
Alex. Walker
Joh. Walker
Joseph Walker
Cha. Hays

Jab. Anderson
Joh. Anderson
Jams. Anderson
Isaac Anderson
And. Hays
John McCroseree
Will. Buchanan
Edw. Boyle
Will. Humphrey
Rich. Courser
Sam. Dunlap
Will. Louchrage
Rob. Dunlap
Jams. Ecken

Will. Mitchell
Natha. Evins
John Stephenson
Jas. Eken
Jas. Greeblee
John Paul
Mat. Lyle
Joh. Gray
Ths. McSpedan
Joh. Mathews
Will. Armstrong
Rob. Huddon
Will. Hall
Sam. Gray

And. Martin
John Edmoston
Jas. Robinson
Ths. Duchart
Will. Quin
Thos. Williams

Will. McCoutes
John Moor
Will. Moor
David Moor
Alex. Moor
And. Moor

Isaac Taylor
Michel O'Docherty
Sam. McClewer
Natha. McClewer
John Philipmayer

Company No. 3.

James Cathey, Capt.
John Given
John Case
Andr. Carl
Will. Brown
David Logan
John Case
Sam. Case
Thos. Stephenson
David Stephenson
John McClewer
Joseph Hanna
John Frame
John King
Hugh Camble

Robert Joweter
Michel Dickey
Rob. Brown
Nichol Leeper
Rob. McDowel
Sam Hues
Wm. Hains
Rob. Craig
James Allan
Wm. Monson
James Chambers
Wm. Johnston
Sam. Givens
James Givens
Thos. Lander

David Nelson
Archibel Hamilton
Rob. Koney
James Fowler
Edw. Givens
James Case
Georg. Anderson
Nathan Underwood
Georg. Anderson
James Scot
Andr. Cathey
Fracs. Raley
John McCown

Company No. 4.

John Christian, Capt.
Wm. Christian, Lieut.

Fran. Betty, Ensign

John Holms
Josep Reed
Finley McClewer
Georg. Camble
Georg. Caldwell
Wm. Caldwell
Alex. Thompson
Jas. Caldwell
Isaac McCulough
Jas. Armstrong
Wm. Armstrong
Thos. Henderson
Wm. Henderson
Rob. Conigham
Wm. Conigham
Thos. Black
Wm. Johnston
Joh. Davison
And. Cowin
Jas. Moody
Jas. Willson
Niol. Leeper
Jno. Turk
Wm. Adams

David Mitchel
Rob. Ramsay
Georg. Breackinred
Jno. Mitchel
Jno. Doake
Sam. Doake
Patt. Hayes
And. Boyd
Jas. Fulton
John Fulton
John Brownlee
Chas. Camble
Jas. Camble
Will. Camble
Jno. Buchanan
Nathan McClewer
Jas. Robinson
Antho. Black
Will. Lang
Thos. Bell
Jas. Bell
Jno. Black
Jas. Black
Wm. Robinson

John Robinson
Thos. Shields
Alx. Fordice
And. McCord
Jas. Beans
Thos. Beans
Anth. Hamilton
David Steel
Rob. Alexander
And. Scot
Morris Thompson
John Maxwell
Ths. Lewis
Pat. Barney
Alex. Brackinredg
Rob. Brackinredg
Jas. Brackinridg
—— McCoulough
Jas. Miller
Rob. McClenachon
John Thompson
And. Russel
Rand McDonel
Hug. Martin

Company No. 5.

Peter Showll, Capt.
And. Burd, Lieut.

Math. Skeens, Ensign

Abram Harden	Griffiths Thomas	Thos. Moor
John Hill	Wm. White	John Hodg
Johnath. Burley	John White	Stephanes Harworth
John Harison	Isaac Lotos	Absolum Harworth
Georg. Clemens	Adam Sherral	Jas. Harworth
Wm. Halimes	Wm. Sherral	John Harworth
Benj. Haws	Rob. Caldwal	John Reeson
Zebulan Harrison	Volante Severe	Steph. Howard
John Harrison	John Miller	Absolum Howard
Jno. Davis	John Cumberland	Joseph Howard
Jno. Taylor	Will. Briges	John Benson
Thos. Lawker	Jacob Jacobs	
Joseph Burley	Wm. Carrel	

Company No. 6.

James Gill, Capt.

John Dobin, Lieut

Wm. Sharrell	Jno. Fisher	Sam. Brown
Rans. Harding	John Hawlain	John McClairn
Wm. Willing	Ths. Wilkins	John Cumberland
John Johnson	And. Holman	Wm. Sharrle, Sr.
John Wilkins	Joseph Harding	Wm. Sharrle, Jr.
Georg. Furbush	Georg. Legler	Sam Beason
Barnaber McHenery	John Ryal	James Spencer
Rich. Dictum	Joseph Dunham	Wm. Pricket
Cornleus Dan. Murley	Abram Dunklederey	Wm. Hall
Nicol. Cain	Timothy Taylor	Wm. McClain
Nicola. Brock	Riley Moor	Michel Brock
Henry Brock	Georg. Willes	Thos. West
Martin Shoemaker	Fradrich Brock	Wm. Sames

Company No. 7.

John Wilson, Capt.	Morace Offral	David Camble
Sam McCallhison	Sa. Walace	Jas. Lockard
Nathan Luck	Rob. Davies	Kno. McCutcheon
John Shields	John Spear	Wm. McCutcheon
John Green	Jno. Brown	Jas. McCutcheon
John Patterson	Thos. Peery	Rob. McCutcheon
Georg. Davidson	Wm. McClantok	Alex. Crocket
Jno. Hunter	Alex. McCorrel	Wm. Camble
Wm. Hunter	Wm. Johnston	Nathaniel Davis
Jas. Hunter	Rob. Young	James Philip
Jno. Rusk	Jno. Young	Jno. Barkley
Jas. Clark	Jas. Young	Jas. Luck
Wm. Vance	Hugh Young	Jas. Tramble
Rob. Crocket	Jacob Lockard	Benj. Walker
John Trumble	Ths. Kirkpatrick	Wm. Leadgerwood
Wm. King	Patt. Cook	

Company No. 8.

George Robinson, Capt.
Jas. McFeron, Lieut.
Pat. Shirky, Ensign
Jas. Ranfro, Serj.

Dan. Mananghan
Mark Eval
Peter Ranfro
Georg. Draper
Rob. Roland
Edm. Smith
Fran. Kelly
And. Gaughagall
Henry Stiles
Hen. Philip
Ths. Looney
Rob. Looney
Dan. Looney
Adm. Looney
Mark Joans

Jno. Smith
Jno. Askins
Hugh Caruthers
Jno. Flower
Wm. Bradshay
Jas. Coal
Jno. Coal
Bryan Cass
Wm. Craven
Cornel. Dougherty
Simon Acres
Wm. Acres
Nicol. Horsford
Josh. Tasker
—— Mealore

Hen. Brown
Sam. Brown
Jas. Burk
Wm. Bean
—— Evins
Sam. Martin
Peter Kinder
Stevan Evens
Peter Watkins
Stephen Ranfro
Benj. Davis
Wm. Clark
Wm. Sheperd
Benj. Dearon

Company No. 9.

John McDowel, Capt.
Jas. McDowel
Ephe. McDowel
David Dreden
Alex. McClewr
Jono. McClewr
Holbert McClewr
Sam. McRoberts
Thos. Taylor
Jno. McKnab
And. McKnab
Thos. Whiteside
Jno. Aleson
David Bires
Alex. McClure
Jno. Gray

Moses McClure
Patt. McKnab
Jno. Cosier
Wm. Hall
Erwin Patterson
Edw. Patterson
Jno. Miles
Jos. Finey
Jas. Harderman
Chas. Quail
Sam. Wood
Wm. Wood
Rich. Wood
Hen. Hirkam
Josp. Lapsley
Gilbert Camble

Jas. Camble
Rob. Young
Math. Young
—— Long
Jas. More
Hugh Cuningham
Jas. Cuningham
Jno. Cares
Fran. McCowen
Hum. Beaker
Jno. Peter Paley
Mich. Miller
Loromor Mason
Jno. Mathews

Source: Draper MSS., Hist. Soc. of Wisconsin.

Miscellaneous County Rosters.

MILITIA OFFICERS CHARLES CITY COUNTY.
Sept. 17, 1655.

Col. Edwd. Hill
Lieut.-Col. Walter Aston
Capt. Richard Tye

Capt. Daniel Peibles
Capt. Wm. Harris
Capt. Danl. Lewellin

July 2, 1661.

Col Abraham Wood
Lieut.-Col. Thos. Drewe
Major Miller Harris
Capt. John Epes
Source: Order Book.

Capt. Edward Hill
Capt. Francis Gray
Capt. Thos. Stegge,
    Commander of Horse.

COUNTY MILITIA.--RANGERS.
James City, Jan. 13, 1692.

Giles Webb, Lieut.
Thomas Smith, Lieut.
Source: Va. State Papers, Vol. I, p. 32.

John Taliaferro, Lieut.
David Straughan, Lieut.

LANCASTER COUNTY MILITIA, 1656

Att a court helde at James Cittie the 13th of December, 1656.

Colonel, John Carter
Lieut.-Colonel, Hen. Fleete
Source: Va. Mag., Vol. 8, p. 177.

Major, Tho. Bries

RETURN OF FIELD OFFICERS FOR ELIZABETH CITY CO.
November 22, 1752.

John Hunter, Col.
John Tabb, Major of Horse
Robt. Armistead, Major of Foot
Source: Va. State Papers, V. I, p. 247.

Cary Selden, Capt.
Chas. King, Capt.
Westwood Armistead, Capt.

LIST OF OFFICERS IN ESSEX COUNTY.
April 9, 1753.

John Corbin, Col. of Militia
Thos. Waring, Col. of Horse
Wm. Dangerfield, Col. of Foot

Fran. Smith, Major of Horse
Wm. Roan, Major of Foot

Captains.

Forest Upshaw   Fra. Waring   Wm. Garnett
James Jones   Rich. Tyler   Saml. Hipkins
Wm. Covington   Thos. Edmundson   Simon Miller

Source: Va. State Papers, Vol. I, p. 247.

FAUQUIER COUNTY.

May 24, 1759. Joseph Blackwell. Sheriff; Henry Churchill, Esq., Co. Lieutenant.

Aug. 23, 1759. William Blackwell, Colonel; William Eustace, Major.

Sept. 27, 1759. John Bell, Colonel; Elias Edmonds, William Wright, Armistead Churchill, John James, Augustine Jennings, Thomas McClanahan and Robert Ashby, Captains.

March 27, 1760. Simon Miller, Captain; George Bennet, Thomas Watts, William Howell, James Foley, Lieutenants.

June 27, 1760. William Little, Captain.

Oct. 23, 1760. Howson Kenner, Captain ; James Seaton, Lieutenant.

Nov. 28, 1760. Henry Mauzy, Lieutenant.

April 23, 1761. Thomas Harrison, County Lieutenant ; John Bell, Colonel; William Eustace, Major.

May 28, 1761. John Bell, Sheriff.

June 26, 1761. William Blackwell, Colonel ; John James, Robert Ashby, Captains.

July 23, 1761. George Kenner, Thomas McClanahan, Augustine Jennings, Captains ; Jacob Rector, Ensign.

July 23, 1761. William Little, Captain ; Henry Mauzy, Lieutenant ; Peter Kampser, Ensign.

Aug. 27, 1761. Thomas Marshall, James Scott, Captains ; James Seaton, William Conway, Lieutenants; Original Young, Burdit Clifton, Ensigns.

Sept. 24, 1761. Nimrod Ashby, Captain.

Nov. 26, 1761. Simon Miller, Captain ; George Bennit, Lieutenant ; James Foley, Thomas Garner, Ensigns.

March 25, 1762. Martin Pickett, Bailey Johnson, Lieutenants ; William Norris, Timothy Stamps, William Neavil, Ensigns.

May 27, 1762. Howson Kenner, Major.

June 25, 1762. James Seaton, Captain.

May 26, 1763. William Grant, Esq., Sheriff.

Sept. 22, 1763. John Gibson, Captain ; Peter Grant, Thomas Raley, Lieutenants.

Sept. 27, 1764. James Bell, Captain.

Nov. 24, 1766. John Moffett, Captain.

July 28, 1767. Charles Morehead, Captain ; John Chilton, Lieutenant.

March 26, 1770. Augustine Jennings, Major.

April 23, 1770. William Eustace, Colonel ; Thomas Helm, Captain.

May 28, 1770. Paul Williams, Lieutenant.

Oct. 22, 1770. John Ashby, Jr., Captain.

May 24, 1773. Nicholas George, Captain; Richard Covington, Lieutenant.

Source : Order Books.

FAUQUIER COUNTY

Roster of Captain Wm. Edmond's company of Virginia troops in the French and Indian war, 1761.

Martin Pickett, Lieut.	Joseph Hollsclaw	John Hitt
Wm. Ransdale	Alex. Jeffries	Joseph Hitt
Wm. Norris, Ensign	Stephen Bailey, Patrowler	Thos. Jackman, Jnr.
Simon Morgan, Serg.	Danl. Triplett	Jeffrey Johnston
Edmond Baisley, Serg.	Wm. White	Herrman Hitt
Thos. Porter, Serg.	Hugh Jaquitt	Wm. M. Penison
John Baisley, Serg.	Jos. Carter	Jno. Morgan
Saml. Simpson, Corp.	Charles Martin	Wm. Pickett, Jnr.
Edw. Ball, Corp.	Henry Boatman	Thos. McClanahan
Humphrey Arnold, Corp.	Jas. Oliver	Wm. Smith, Jnr.
Joseph Smith	George Herrin	Richard Jackman
Wm. Underwood	James Pendleton	John Russell
Wm. Smith, Snr.	Jno. Pickett	Wm. Bragg
John Miller	John Hitt, Jnr.	John Boden
Thos. Smith	Jno. Hitt, son of Joseph	Wm. Russell
Wm. Robertson	Wm. Gibson	Carr Bailey
Henry Martin	Simon Morgan	Wm. Willson
Chattin Lampkin	Law Taylor	John Blackwell
James Lampkin	Jos. Taylor	Jas. Bailey
Thomas Bell	John Baisey	Peter Taylor
James Bell	Jos. Hudnall	Jas. Morgan
William Ball	Jno. Hudnall, Patrowler	Charles Garner
James Jeffries	Wm. Norriss	John Duncan, Jnr.

Thos. Harrison, County Lieut. Sept. 25, 1761.

Source: Va. Hist. Mag. V. 7, p. 305.

ISLE OF WIGHT CO. MILITIA.

At a Court held Nov. 5th, 1772.

Timothy Tines, Major	James Bridger, Capt.
John Scarsbrook Wills, Captain	Henry Harrison, Capt.
Benj. Applewhaite, Capt.	Benjamin Ely, Lieut.
John Lawrence, Capt.	James Wills, Lieut.

In the militia of this county, severally took the oaths, etc.

Source: Order Book.

LIST OF OFFICERS IN KING AND QUEEN COUNTY.
June 12, 1707.

Col. John Lightfoot	Capt. John Collier (foot)
Col. John Walker	Capt. John Gyly (foot)
Major John Lee (horse)	Capt. James Wood (foot)
Capt. John Major (horse)	Capt. Thos. Walker
Capt. Jeremiah Clowdes (horse)	Lieut. Rich. Norshaw Walker
Capt. Thomas Pettit (dragoons)	Cornet James Walker
Capt. Thos. Tunstall (dragoons)	

Source: Va. State Papers, Vol. I, p. 114.

MIDDLESEX COUNTY MILITIA, JULY 10, 1676.

David Hume, Lieut.
Richard Duerdine, Corpl.

John Hunter, Sergt.
Thomas Dring, Corpl.

Privates.

Walter Doconly
James Gray
William Rane
William Forbus (Forbes)
John Davis
Edward Ellis
Thomas Little
Cornelius Lane
John Hackley

Edward Clarke
William Wright
James Theste
William Cottrell
Henry Griffith
John Simpson
Hugh Roberts
William Harris
William Wood

Danl. Hargrove
Charles Sheppard
Richard Bishopp
John Tembed
Thomas Smith
Patrick Mitchell
Philip Tanxey
Thomas Stone

Horsemen.

Ralph Whitten, Corpl.
Thomas Jackson
Source: Order Book.

William Sumers
Thomas Smith

MIDDLESEX COUNTY MILITIA, 1687.

Att a Court held for the County of Middlesex the 23rd day of November, 1687. Present :

Coll. Christopher Wormeley, Captain Walter Whitaker, Mr. John Wortham, Mr. Oswald Carey, Mr. William Daniell.

The Court being mett together by vertue of his Excelees. Commands Signified by his letter of the 14th Instant to take an Accot. of what men in the County are Capable to finde horse and men, as likewise to serve on Foot in the Militia of this County. Upon full examination of the same doe hereby make returne as followeth :

That the Persons whose names are underwritten are by this Court thought of Sufficient abilitie to finde a Man, horse and Armer :

James Blaze
Mr. Doodes Minor
Mr. Maurice Cock
William Montague
Mr. Randelph Seager
Jeremy Avery
Tho. Lee
Mr. Robt. Price
Mr. Abrah. Weekes
Mr. Tho. Corbin
John Nash
Mr. Francis Weekes
Thomas Tazeley
John Rickins
George Goodloe
Marvill Moseley

Mr. John Willis
Mr. Henry Thacker
John Jeffreys, Esq.
Thos. Williams
Mr. Charles Curtis
Mr. John Nicholls
Col. Christr. Wormeley
Mr. Robert Boodle
Coll. John Armistead
Widdow Batcheldor
Mr. Alexander Smith
Mr. Tho. Stapleton
Edward Clarke
Mr. John Wortham
Mr. Richard Robertson
Mr. Christopher Robinson

Mr. Job Vause
Mr. William Nicholson
Mr. Henry Nicholls, Jr.
Mr. Henry Wood
Mr. George Reeves
Mr. John Cant
Ralph Wormeley, Esq.
Mr. Joseph Goare
Mr. Robert Dudley
Mr. John Needles
Mr. Tho. Hill
Tho. Townsend
Mr. Will Churchill
Mr. Christopher Kilbell
Mr. James Curtis
Mr. Max Petty
Wm. Brooks, Trumpetter

And they say Upon further Examination that the persons underwritten are thought by this Court Capable to Serve as footmen and to finde themselves with Armes.

Henry Osborne	John Stamper	William Carter
John Summers, Drummer	William Woodward	Richard Gabriell
Thomas Edgecock	William Downing	John Goodrich
Antho. Daughton	John Smith,	Tho. Guy
John Lohil	Mrs. Weatherby's son	John Beamont
George Guest	Nicholas Rice	Andrew Williamson
Tho. Paine	Thomas Munns	William Lloyall
Robert Poste	Thomas Thompson	John Skeer
John Brumm	Peter Brummell	Peter Chelton
William King	Patrick Miller	Thomas Norman
Thomas Wood	William Tignor	John Vivion
John Gutteridge	Robert Gillian	Tho. Cranke
John Micham	Augustine Scarborow	Francis Dodson
Richard Allen	William Dudley	John Else
Thomas Crispe	John Sutton	Willis Humphreys
John Brewer	William Thompson	James Bendall
James Ingram	William Beamont	Ezekiah Rhodes
Thomas Kidd	William Barber	John Sandford
Robert Williamson	John Ross	Thomas Gardiner
Robert Blakey	Tho. Stiff	George Woolley
William Mullins	John Bell	James Dudley
Abraham Brierly	John Bristow	Tho. Dudley
Nicho. Paine	Tho. Blewford	David Barwick
John Furrill	Nicho. West	William Sheppard
Richard Reynolds	Edward Dorker	James Pate
John Parsons	Robert Chewning	Francis Fragoe
Alex. Murray	Nicholas Fowle	Thos. Wetherston
	George Pristuall	Michaell Musgrave

NORTHAMPTON COUNTY, 1651.

The following were appointed to command the military districts at a Court, May 10, 1651.

Capt. Stephen Charlton of Nassawattocks.
Capt. Edmund Scarborough of Occohannock.
Capt. Saml. Goldsmith of Nandue.
Capt. Wm. Andrews of Hungars.
Capt. John Stringer of Savage's Neck.
Capt. Obedience Robins.
Capt. Edward Douglas of Magotha Bay.
Capt. Peter Walker to command the Horse.

The following were appointed to command the military districts or precincts of Northampton, 9th of October, 1651.

From lower end of Magotha Bay to south side of Old Plantation Creek, Captain Edward Douglas.
For regiment of Horse, Captain Peter Walker.
From the house of Lewis Whyte to Old Plantation Creek, including John Little's house at Seaside, Major Obedience Robins.

From house of Lewis Whyte including Savage's Neck, Captain John Savage.
For Hungars Creek, Captain William Andrews.
For Nuswattocks Creek, Captain Stephen Charlton.
For Occahomock Creek, Captain Edmund Scarburgh.
For precincts of Nandua, Captain Samuel Goldsmith.

Source : Northampton Court Rec., Vols. 3 and 4,

OFFICERS OF NORTHUMBERLAND COUNTY MILITIA
July 4, 1676.

Col. Codd
Lieut.-Col. Saml. Smyth
Major Thos. Brereton
Capt. Jno. Rogers

Capt. Leod. Howson
Capt. Mattrone
Capt. Peter Knight

NORTHUMBERLAND COUNTY, 20 September, 1676.

The following officers have been in ye service since 11th of July.

Capt. And. Morton
Lieut. Jno. Browne
Serj. Jno. Phillips

Serj. Jno. Trape
Drummer, Jno. Payne

Source : William & Mary Quarterly, Vol. 8, pp. 25, 27.

RAPPAHANNOCK COUNTY, 1656.

Att a grand Assembly helde at James Cittie, 11th December, 1656.

Colonel Moore Fauntleroy
Lieut.-Colonel Toby Smith
Major Tho. Goodrich

Captain William Underwood
Captain Fra. Slaughter
Captain Richard Lees

Va. Mag, V. 8, No. 2, p. 177.

RICHMOND COUNTY ORDER BOOK.

Applications for pay for services rendered by the Militia, under date of March 6, 1704–5 :

Wm. Tayloe, Colonel & Commander in Chief
Captain Thomas Beale
Captain John Craske

Captain William Barber
Captain Henry Brereton
Captain John Tarpley
Captain Charles Barber

October, 1704

Captain William Underwood
Captain Nicholas Smith

Captain Alexander Donaphan

October 2, 1713,

Colonel John Tayloe
Lieut.-Col. Charles Barber
Captain John Tarpley, Jr.
Captain James Ingo

Captain Robert Tomlin
Capt. Newman Brockenbrough
Lieut. James Russell
Lieut. John Morton

Lieut. Thomas Barber
Lieut. Francis Dowman
Cornet Thomas Nash
Cornet Henry Wilson

Qualified in their respective commissions by taking the required oaths.

Source : Order Book.

MILITIA IN SURRY COUNTY IN 1687.

"This Court having considered the Capacitie and abilities of the severall Freeholders and Inhabitants of this county doe most humbly present his Excellency the following persons for horse and ffoott as they are here severall set downe." Ordr. of Council dated 8 br. ye 24th, 1687.

For Horse.

Col. Phill. Ludwell, a man and horse
John Thompson
Tho. Collier
Walter Flood
Tho. Flood
John Watkins, Capt.
Roger Potter
Wm. Foreman
Tho. Binns
Tho. Warren
Geo. Williams
Tho. High
Samll. Thompson
Jno. Edwards
James Jordan
River Jordan
Jno. King

Wm. Simons
Tim. Essell, Junr.
Tho. Bentley, Junr.
Tho. Jolly
Wm. Carpinter
Jno. Barker
Tho. Tias
Wm. Hunt
Wm. Rose
Tho. Bage
Xto. Foster
Ni. Meriwether
Antho. Hardwicke
Tho. Busby
Jos. Ford
Hen. Tucker
Tho. Drew
Robert Lancaster

Tho. Jarrett
Tim. Walker
Ni. Sessorms
Wm. Gwathney
Math. Swann
Wm. Chambers
Wm. Gray
Wm. Newsume
Wm. Newit
Jno. Holt
Wm. Hancock
Rogr. Delke
Charles Jarrett
Wm. Seward, a Quaker
Tho. Partridge, a Quaker
Walter Bartlett, a Quaker
Jno. Barnes, a Quaker

For Foot.

Sion Hill
Danll. Regan
Rogr. Williams
Law. Fleming
Ja. Byneham
Geo. Blow
John Byneham
David Beard
Jno. Golledge
Fra. Sowerby
Cha. Merrett
Wm. Draper
Jno. Steward
Rich. Judkins, Junr.
Joshua Proctor
Robert Owen
Wm. Rogers
Jno. Drew
Wm. Foster
Wm. Howell
Jno. Lathar
Wm. Gray

Nat. Dennis
Tho. Presson
Jethro Barker
Hincha Gillum
Jno. Rankins
Jno. Collier
Wm. Blackborne
Jer. Ellis, Junr.
Wm. Wheeler
Tho. Peddington
Jno. Battle
Ja. Watkins
Max Mansell
Jno. Rogers
Robt. Nathan
Jno. Wallis
Jarvis Newton
Rich. Smith
Wm. Harrington
Ja. Porch
Tho. Farmer
Ja. Morish

Ja. Ely
Wm. Cockerham
Tho. Wolves, a Quaker
Jno. Shugar
Tho. Waller
Ja. Bruton
Tho. Wright
Antho. Evans
Wm. Bruton
Jno. Page
Wm. Blith
Tho. Lane, Junr.
Bray Hargrave
Tho. Futrill
Jno. Clarke
Wm. Rugsbee
Rogr. Gilbert
Jno. Phillips
Wm. Creede
Ja. Hugate
Tho. Browne
Robt. Hart

Jno. Spitless
Wm. Crews
Walter Tompkins
Wm. Wray
Wm. Petway
Jno. Fiveash
Robt. Warren
Allen Warren
Peter Deberry
Jno. Clarke
Wm. Rivers
Tho. Kersey
Tho. Andrews, Junr.
Robt. Andrews
Bat. Andrews
Cha. Digby
Fra. Regan
Edwd. Booky
John Higgs
Jonah Bennett
Daniel Andrews
Tho. Ironmonger
Wm. Nash
Law. Meazle
Humphrey Felps
Robt. Dolling
Tho. Sidway
Patrick Lashly
Geo. Jordan
Jno. Allen
Peter Bayley
Jno. Middleton
Geo. Nichollson
Jno. Wilkinson
Wm. Tillinsworth
Adam Heath
Wm. Harvy
Cha. Briggs
Jno. Roberts
Wm. Dennis
Richard Greene
Tho. Wiggins
Richard Hyde
Tho. Hayward
Noah Barefoot
Jno. Pulesson
Geo. Huson
Robt. Judkins
Blewit Beamont
Cha. Judkins
Tho. Forbush

Owen Mirick
Jno. Garner
Jno. Sharpe
Robt. Austin
Tho. Battle
Jno. Warpool
Wm. Houlford
Tho. Hux
Tho. Adkins
Rich. Adkins
Ja. Jolly
Robt. Nichollson
Hen. Wych
Walter Cotten
Joell Barker
Tho. Blunt
Henry Briggs
Wm. Horniford
Jos. Wall
Robt. Littlebery
Jno. Brown
Ja. Kilpatrick
Tho. Ward
Jno. Gray
Roger Nicholls
Richard Jackson
Jno. Rodwell
Wm. Jackson
Daniel Rich
Robert Craford
Jonah Hickman
Jno. Kindred
Rich. Moonk
Austin Hunnicutt
Jno. Berryman
Wm. Also
Nathan Joyce
Daniell Harryson
Jeoffry Busby
Nathl. Hales
Bat. Figgus
David Phillips
Rich. Jones
Hez. Bunnell
Hen. Norton
Tho. Perice
Cha. Savage
Tho. Mathars
Rogr. Squier
Hen. Baker
Geo. Morrell, a Quaker

Rich. Shaw
Rich. Peirce
Edwd. Nubee
Michael Essell
Geo. Essell
Edw. Taylor
Robert Inman
Tho. Edwards,
   of Hog Island
Edwd. Runee
Tho. Cockerham
Tho. Cooke
Tho. Cotten
Edwd. Grantum
Tho. Sowersby
Cha. White
Luke Mizle
Rich Jordan, Senr.
Wm. Knott
Edwd. Greene
Tho. Blunt
Jer. Ellis, Senr.
Tho. Deerkin
Rich Beighton
Robt. Flake, Junr.
Jos. Richardson
Ar. Davies, Senr.
Wm. Holt
Wm. Goodman
Phill. Shelley
Jos. Thorpe, Junr.
Dennis Rethden
Robt. Lacy, a Quaker
Robert Renolls
Michael Upchurch
Tho. Harebottle
Ja. Griffin
Jno. Greene
Ar. Davis, Junr.
Jos. Lane
John Little
Jno. Procter
Jno. Davies
Wm. Cocke
Robert Reddick
Cha. Goodrich
Josias Wood
Ja. Horsnell
Wm. Crouch
Wm. Peacock
Robt. Fellows

Samll. Judkins
Jno. Cowood
Ja. Ellis
Ni. Witherington
Ja. Omoone
Robt. House, Junr.
Tho. Davis
Samll. Cooke
Jno. Phillips,'Junr.
Tho. Horton
Hen. Hart
Jno. Myles
Jno. Clements
Jno. Casse
Jno. Warren

Edwd. Napkin
Wm. Rowland
Wm. Hooker
Ja. Cooke
Wm. Pittman
Tho. Pittman
Nath. Cornish
Tho. Clary
Wm. Clary
Wm. Harris
Jno. Finley
Ch. Williams
Tho. Forver
Joseph Seate

Evan Humphrey
Edwd. Drew
Tho. White
Anselm Bayley
Tho. Hart
Tho. Lane, Senr.
Jno. Dunfeild
Ja. Reddick
Walter Taylor
Jno. Vincent
Hen. Francis
Rich. Washington
Wm. Lucas
Ni. Pasfeild

MILITARY OFFICERS IN VIRGINIA, 1680.

Henrico County.

Col. William Bird
Lieut.-Col. John Ffarrar

Major Tho. Chamberlain
Capt. Wm. Randolph

Charles City County.

Col. Edward Hill
Lieut.-Col. Dan'l. Clarke
Major John Stith
Capt. Robt. Lucy

Capt. Dan'l Lewellin
Capt. John Hamlin
Lieut.-Col. Tho. Grendon, horse
Capt. Wm. Archer, horse

James City County.

Col. Tho. Ballard
Major Saml. Weldon
Capt. Hen. Soanes

Capt. Wm. Hartwell
Capt. Wm. White, horse

Isle of Wight County.

Col. Jos. Bridger, horse
Major J. A. Powell, horse
Col. Arthr. Smith

Major Tho. Taberer
Lieut.-Col. Jno. Pitt
Capt. Jno. Gutridge

Col. Jos. Bridger, Commander in Chief of ye horse in ye Counties of Isle of
Wight, Surrey, Nanzemond and Lower Norfolk.

Surrey County.

Col. Thos. Swann
Lieut.-Col. Wm. Browne
Major Saml. Swan

Capt. Roger Potter
Capt. Chas. Barham, horse

Nanzemond County.

Col. Jno. Lear
Major Bar Kerney
Capt. Andrew Booth, horse

Capt. James Jossey, horse
Lieut.-Col. Tho. Milner
Capt. Tho. Goodwin

Warwick County.

Col. Wm. Cole, horse and foot
Major Hum. Harwood

Capt. Rich. Whitticar
Capt. Jno. Langhorne, horse

Lower Norfolk County.

Col. Lemuell Mason
Lieut.-Col. Robt. Bray
Major Antho. Lawson

Capt. Jno. Niccolls
Capt. Adam Keeling
Capt. Wm. Robinson, horse

Elizabeth City County.

Col. Charles Morrison
Major Matthew Wakelin

Capt. Antho. Armstead, horse

New Kent County.

Col. Jno. West
Lieut.-Col. Geo. Lyddale
Major Martin Palmer
Capt. Wm. Jones

Capt. Brian Smith
Capt. Jno. Lewis, horse
Capt. Rich. Johnson, horse

York County.

Col. Jno. Page
Major Otho Thorp

Capt. Fra. Page
Capt. Jno. Tiplady

Gloucester County.

Col. August Warner
Lieut.-Col. Law Smith
Major Fra. Burrell
Capt. Rich. Booker
Col. Matthew Kemp, horse
Major Hen. Whiteing, horse

Lieut.-Col. Armestead, horse
Capt. Jno. Smith, horse
Col. Tho. Pate
Lieut.-Col. Phill. Lightfoot
Maj. Robt. Payton
Capt. Symond Belford

Rappahannock County.

Col. Jno. Stone
Lieut.-Col. Wm. Loyd
Major Hen. Smith
Capt. Saml. Bromfield

Capt. Danl. Gaines
Col. Leroy Griffin, horse
Capt. Tho. Gouldman, horse

Middlesex County.

Col. Chr. Wormeley
Lieut.-Col. Jno. Burnham

Major Robt. Beverley
Capt. Walter Whitticar, horse

Lancaster County.

Col. Wm. Ball
Lieut.-Col. Jno. Carter
Major Edwd. Dale

Capt. Wm. Ball
Capt. David Fox

Westmoreland County.

Col. Wm. Pierce
Lieut.-Col. Isaac Allerton

Major Tho. Youell
Capt. Antho. Bridges

Col. Richard Lee of the Horse, in ye counties of Westmoreland, Northumberland and Stafford.

Northumberland County.

Col. Tho. Brereton
Lieut.-Col. Saml. Smith
Major John Mattrom

Capt. Leonard Housen, horse
Capt. Tho. Mathews
Capt. John Hayne

Stafford County.

Col. Geo. Mason
Lieut.-Col. Cadwalader Jones

Major Andrew Gilson
Capt. Robt. Massey

Northampton County.

Col. John Custis
Col. John Stringer
Lieut.-Col. Wm. Waters
Major. Wm. Spencer

Capt. Wm. Whittington, horse
Col. Jno. Robins
Capt. Fra. Piggott
Capt. Hancock Lee

Accomac County.

Col. Wm. Kendoll
Lieut.-Col. John West
Major Chas. Scarborough

Capt. Edmund Scarborough
Capt. Danl. Jenifer
Capt. Obedience Jonson

Horse.

Col. John Custis
Major Edmund Bouman

Capt. Rich. Hill
Capt. Wm. Custis

Source: Colonial Papers of Virginia, No. 63, British State Paper Office.

VIRGINIA MILITIA OFFICERS, 1699.

Taken from the MS. records of the Virginia Council, December 9, 1698, to May 20, 1700, now deposited in the Congressional Library.

June 3, 1699.

Henrico.

William Byrd, Colonel and Commander in Chief; William Randolph, Lieutenant-Colonel; Peter Field, Major.

Charles City.

Edward Hill, Colonel and Commander in Chief; Edward Hill, Jr., Lieutenant-Colonel; Charles Goodrich, Major.

Surrey.

Benjamin Harrison, Colonel and Commander in Chief; Henry Tooker, Major.

Isle of Wight.

Samuel Bridger, Lieutenant-Colonel and Commander in Chief; Henry Baker, Major.

Nansemond.

George Norsworthy, Lieutenant-Colonel and Commander in Chief; Thomas Swann, Major.

Princess Anne.

Anthony Lawson, Lieutenant-Colonel and Commander in Chief; John Thoroughgood, Major.

Norfolk.

Lemuel Mason, Lieutenant Colonel and Commander in Chief; James Wilson, Major.

Elizabeth City.

William Wilson, Lieutenant-Colonel and Commander in Chief; Anthony Armistead, Major.

Warwick.

Miles Cary, Lieutenant-Colonel and Commander-in-Chief; William Cary, Major.

James City.

Philip Ludwell, Colonel and Commander in Chief; Henry Duke, Lieutenant-Colonel.

York.

Edmund Jenings, Colonel and Commander in Chief: Thomas Ballard, Lieutenant-Colonel; William Buckner, Major.

New Kent.

John Lightfoot, Colonel and Commander in Chief; Joseph Foster, Lieutenant-Colonel; William Bassett, Major.

King and Queen.

William Leigh, Colonel and Commander in Chief; Joshua Story, Major.

Gloucester.

Matthew Page, Colonel and Commander in Chief; James Ransom, Lieutenant-Colonel; Peter Beverley, Major.

Middlesex.

Ralph Wormeley, Colonel and Commander in Chief; Matthew Kemp, Lieutenant-Colonel; Robert Dudley, Major,

Essex.

Ralph Wormeley, Colonel and Commander in Chief; William Moseley, Lieutenant-Colonel; John Catlett, Major.

Lancaster.

Robert Carter, Colonel and Commander in Chief; Joseph Ball, Lieutenant-Colonel.

Northumberland.

Robert Carter, Colonel and Commander in Chief; George Cowper, Lieutenant-Colonel; Rodham Kenner, Major.

Westmoreland.

Richard Lee, Colonel and Commander in Chief; Willoughby Allerton, Lieutenant-Colonel; Francis Wright, Major.

Richmond.

Richard Lee, Colonel and Commander in Chief; George Taylor, Lieutenant-Colonel; Thomas Lloyd, Major.

Stafford.

George Mason, Lieutenant-Colonel and Commander in Chief; Thomas Owsley, Major.

Accomack.

Charles Scarborough, Colonel and Commander in Chief; Richard Bayley, Major.

Northampton.

John Custis, Colonel and Commander in Chief; Nathaniel Littleton, Lieutenant-Colonel; William Waters, Major.

VOLUNTEER CAVALRY ASSOCIATION, 1756.

Williamsburg, May 28. On Thursday the 20th, several Gentlemen of the Association, under Colonel Peyton Randolph, met at Fredericksburg to the number of 130, and at a Council of War held next day the following Gentlemen were chosen officers, viz.:

Captains.

Warner Lewis   Richard Eppes
Bernard Moore   Nathaniel West Dandridge
Charles Carter   John Syme

Aides-de-Camp.

Presley Thornton   Charles Osborne
Source: Maryland Gazette, June 17, 1756.

The Virginia Regiment.

COMMISSIONS SENT TO COLONEL WASHINGTON FOR THE OFFICERS OF HIS VIRGINIA REGIMENT, 1754.

Adam Stephens,	- - - - -	Lt.-Col., July 20
Robt. Stobo,	- - - - -	Major, July 20
Peter Hogg,	- - - - -	Capt., Mar. 9
Andw. Lewis,	- - - - -	" Mar. 18
Geo. Mercer,	- - - - -	" June 4
Tho. Wagener,	- - - - -	" July 20,
Wm. Polson,	- - - - -	" July 21
Wm. Peyronney,	- - - - -	" Aug. 25
John Savage,	- - - - -	Lieut., Mar. 9
James Towers,	- - ' -	" June 9
Wm. Bronaugh,	- - - -	" July 20
John Mercer,	- - - - -	" July 21
James Craick (acting Surgeon),	- -	" July 23
Wm. Wright,	- - - - -	Ensign, July 20, Lieut., Oct. 28
Carolus Gustavus de Spildolph,	- -	" July 21, " Oct. 29
Thos. Bullet,	- - - - -	" July 22, " Oct. 30
Walter Stewart,	- - - -	" July 25, " Aug. 31

Source : Dinwiddie Papers : Vol. I., p. 319.

MEMORANDUM LIST OF OFFICERS IN THE VIRGINIA REGIMENT, 1754, WITH THEIR PAY SEVERALLY.

Col. Joseph Fry, Com'dr-in-Chief, 15s. per day and £100 per annum for his table.

George Washington, Esq., Lieut.-Colonel, - - - - -	12s. 6d.
Muse, Major, - - - - . - - - -	10s.
Wm. Trent, Captain, - - - - - - - -	8s.
Adam Stephen Captain, - - - - - - - -	8s.
Robert Stobo, Captain, - - - - - - - -	8s.
Peter Hogg, Captain, - - - - - - - -	8s.
Andrew Lewis, Captain, - - - - - - -	8s.
Jacob Vanbraam, Lieutenant, - - - - -	4s.
Geo. Mercer, Lieutenant, - - - - - -	4s.
Thos. Wagener, Lieutenant, - - - - - -	4s.
Wm. Polson, Lieutenant, - - - - - -	4s.
John West, Jr., Lieutenant, - - - - - -	4s.
John Savage, Lieutenant, - - - - - -	4s.
James Craik, Surgeon, - - - - - - -	4s.

Source : Dinwiddie Papers. Vol.II., p. 112.

LIST OF OFFICERS

entitled to land under the Proc. of Gov. Dinwiddie, their Assessment to cover the Expenses of Surveys to secure the Lands, and a List of Balances due from Sundrys on Account of their Claims to Land under the Proc. of 1754. (From Col. Geo. Washington's Ledger.)

Estate of Col. Joseph Fry,			£54.11.4
Col. Adam Stephen, Pd.,			11.6.1
Col. Geo. Muse, Paid,			
Estate of Captain Robert Stobo,			46.6.7
Col. Andrew Lewis, Pd.,			12.9.9
Capt. Peter Hog,	C. Craw'd		11.6.½
Capt. Jacob Vanbraam,			40.6.7
Col. Geo. Mercer, Pd. by Mrs. Jas. Mercer,			40.11.11
Mr. Andrew Waggoner,	C. Craw'd,		9.5.3
Mr. John West,	C. Craw'd,		11.9.2
The Estate or Heir of Wm. Polson, C. C.			5.14.10
Lt. John Savage,	C. Craw'd,		20.18.2
Capt. John Bronaugh. Paid,			
Dr. James Craik,	C. Craw'd,		8.3.1
John Baynes, for Jas. Tower's Heirs, C. C.			5.12.2
Heir of Wm. Wright, Paid,			11.4.7
Capt. Thos. Bullet,			11.4.7
Robt. Longdon,	C. C.		2.13.9
Robt. Tunstall,	C. C.		1.12.9
Andr. Waggoner,	C. C.		2.13.9
Richd. Trotter,	C. C.		2.13.9
John David Wilpper			2.13.9
Wire Johnson,	C. C.		2.4.8
Hugh McRoy,	C. C.		2.4.8
Richd. Smith,	C. C.		1.3.8
Chas. Smith,	C. C.		1.15.10
Angus McDonald,	C. C.		1.15.10
Nathan Chapman,	C. C.		1.15.10
Joseph Gatewood,	C. C.		1.15.10
Jas. Samuel,	C. C.		1.15.10
Michael Seally,	C. C.		1.15.10
Edwd. Goodwin,	C. C.		1.15.10
William Baily,	C. C.		1.15.10
Henry Baily,	C. C.		1.15.10
Wm. Copland,	C. C.		1.15.10
Mathew Doran,	C. C.		1.15.10
John Ramsay,			1.15.10
Charles James,			1.15.10
Math. Cox,			1.15.10
Marshall Pratt,			1.15.10
John Wilson,			1.15.10
Wm. Johnston,			1.15.10
Jno. Wilson,			1.15 10
Nathl. Barrett,			14.10
David Gorman,			14.10

Patk. Galloway,	- - - - - - - - - -		£1.15.10
Timothy Conway,	- - - - - - - - - -		
Christian Bombgardner,	. - - - - - - - -		1.15.10
John Maid,	- - - - - - - - - -		1.15.10
John Houston,	- - - - - - - - - -		1.15.10
John Ford,	- - - -	C. C.	- - - - -	1.15.10
Wm. Broughton,	- - -	C. C.	- - - - -	1.15.10
Wm. Carnes,	- - - -	C. C.	- - - - -	1.15.10
Edwd. Evans,	- - - -	C. C.	- - - - -	1.15.10
Thos. Moss,	- - - -	C. C.	- - - - -	1.15.10
Mathew Jones,	- - - -	C. C.	- - - - -	1.15.10
Philip Gatewood,	- - -	C. C.	- - - - -	1.15.10
Hugh Paul,	- - - -	C. C.	- - - - -	1.15.10
Danl. Staples,	- - - -	C. C.	- - - - -	1.15.10
Wm. Lowry,	- - - -	C. C.	- - - - -	1.15.10
James Ludlow,	- - - -	C. C.	- - - - -	
James Lafort,	- - - -	C. C.	- - - - -	
James Gwin,	- - - -	C. C.	- - - - -	
Joshua Jordan,	- - - -	C. C.	- - - - -	
Wm. Jenkins,	- - - -	C. C.	- - - - .	
James Commack,	- - -	C. C.	- - - - -	14.10
Richd. Morris,	- - - -	C. C.	- - - - -	14.10
Jno. Golson,	• - - -	C. C.	- - - - -	14.10
Robt. Jones,	- - - -	C. C.	- - - - -	1.15.10
Wm. Hogan,	- - - - - - - - - -		1.15.10
Jno. Franklin,	- - - - - - - - - -		
John Bishop,	- - - - - - - - - -		
Geo. Malcomb,	- - - - - - - - - -		
Wm. Coleman,	- - - - - - - - - -		
Richd. Bolton,	- - - - - - - - - -		
Jno. Smith,	- - - - - - - - - -		
Geo. Hurst,	- - - -	C. C.	- - - -	
Jno. Cincaid,	- - - -	C. C.	- - - - -	1.15.10
Andrew Fowler,	- - - - - - - - - -		1.15.10
Thos. Napp,	- - - - - - - - - -		1.15.10
The Representatives of Arthur Watts,	- - - - - -		1.15.10
Jno. Fox, Assignee of Jesse May,	- - - - - -		1.15.10
Francis Self,	- - - - - - - - - -		1.15.10
Robt. Stewart,	- - - - - - - - - -		1.15.10
Robt. Murphy,	- - - - - - - - - -		1.15.10
Alexr. Bonny,	- - - - - - - - - -		1.15.10
The Representative of Wm. Horne,	- - - - - •		1.15.10
Wm. McAnulty,	- - - - - - - - - -		1.15.10

Report of the various companies of the Virginia Regiment under the command of Col. Washington made the 9th of July, 1754, at Will's Creek, just after the battle of the Great Meadows.

Return of Captain Stobo's Company, July 9, 1754.

Men Fit for Duty.

James Carson	William Stallons	James Welch
John Goldson	Robert McKoy	Joseph Costerton
John James	Jessy Morris	Henry Bowman
William Coffland	Joseph Gibbs	Henry Neill
David Welch	Anthony Kennedy	John Bryan
Nathaniel Lewis	Charles Waday	Jacob Gowing
John Franklin	Henry Bayly	Benjamin Gause
Adam Jones	William Deweny	John Brown
John Carroll	Nicholas Foster	James Milton
Charles Smith	Jean Moore	William Swallow

Wounded.

Michael McGrath	James Good	Peregrin Williams
Michael Reily	Alexander Stewart	Solomon Botson (deserted)
Patrick Durphy	Robert McCulroy	

Killed in the Engagement.

John Ritson	Thomas Fisher
Daniel McClaran	John Tranton

Left with Sick.

Edward Graves	Richard Morris

Left Lame on Road.

Thomas Langdon (Sergeant)

Sick in Camp.

Robert Tunstile (Sergeant)	James Batty
Dennis Kinton	Thomas Ogden
John Allen	

Absent as Hostage.

Captain Robert Stobo

Source : Force MSS., Library of Congress.

Return of Captain Hog's Company given the 9th of July, 1754.

Men Fit for Duty.

Jesse May	Nicholas Morgan	Zachariah Smith
James Samuel	Thomas Moss	Thomas Napp
Joseph Milton	John Ogilby	Bibby Brooke
Benjamin Hamilton	John Roe	Thomas Slaughter
Matthew Cox	Southey Hazlip	Joseph Gatewood
John Martin	James Thomas	Briant Page

Michael Scully
William Johnston
Abner Hazlip
William Coleman
Thomas Kitson

Peter Effluck
Duncan Farguson
Thomas Chaddwick
John Ramsay
Andrew Fowler

John Meares
Matthew Levison
William Underhill
Thomas Harris

Wounded.

Robert Jones
James Heyter
Mathew Durham
Joshua Burton

Argil House
David Gorman
Robert Elliot
Samuel Hyden

John Chapman
Edward Goodwin
James Ford
Dudley Skinner

Lame on the Road.

Joseph Scott
Marshall Pratt
William Dean

James Letort
Dominick Moran

Left with the Wounded.

Andrew Clark

John Stephens

Sick in the Camp.

Philip Gatewood
   Return made to William Bronough
      Source: Force MSS, Library of Congress.

Return of Captain Lewis's Company, July 9, 1754.

Men Fit for Duty.

John Whitman
John Smith
William Harbinson
Robert Grymes
John Poor
William Poor
Michael McCannon
John Maston
John Biddlecome
Thomas Pearson

Edward Bailey
John Powers
James Ferguson
Jabez Rowe
John Mulholand
Patrick Coyle
John Smith
John Rodgers
Mathew Jones
Joseph Baxter

James Ludlow
Thomas Foster
Thomas Burney
John Burk
Cornelius Henley
William Cranes
Tarance Swinney
James Smith
John Field

Wounded.

Captain Lewis
Lieutenant Savage
John McCulley
James Fulham
John Rodgers

Thomas Bird
Edward Cahell
Arthur Watts
Nehemiah Tendell
John Durham

Thomas Nicholson
Nathan Chapman
Philip Comerly
George McSwine

Killed in Battle.

Thomas Scott
Gerrett Clark

John Ramsay

Left with the Sick.

Josias Baker   Bethow. Burns
Thomas Stedman   Patrick McPick
Robert Murphy   John Truston
James Tytus   Daniel Malatte
John McEntire   James McCormack

Source : Force MSS., Library of Congress.

A list of Captain Van Braam's Company, July 9, 1754.

Killed.

John Robinson   William Bailey
William Simmons

Wounded.

John Hamilton (Sergeant)   John Potter
Rudol. Brickner (Sergeant)   Joseph Powell
Wile Johnston   Dernsey Simmons
George Taylor

Sick in Camp.

William Gerrard

Sick on the Road.

Robert Bell   Richard Bolton
George Merharren

On Command.

Thomas Dunahough   Michael Franks

Absent.

William Knowls   Nicholas Major
James Black   Godfrey Bombgarden
John Brown

Men Fit for Duty.

Thomas Carter (Sergeant)   John Campbell   Thomas Hennessy
John Allen (Corporal)   Edward King   Francis Rogers
Esechial Richardson (Drummer)   John Coin
Christopher Byarly   Charles Dunn   Edward Whitehead
William Mitchell   Patrick Galloway   Hugh Paul
John Stewart   Jacob Funkhowser   Angus McDonald
John McGuire   Barnard Draxeller   Arthur Howard
Charles Allbury   George Gobell   Mathias Sharp
Francis Self   William Carter   Edward Minor
John Johnston   John Thomson   Benjamin Spiser
        Per John Mercer, Ensign.

Source : Force MSS., Library of Congress.

A return of Captain Mercer's Company, July 9, 1754.

Fit for Duty.

James Tyrrel   William Field   Christopher Bombgardner
John Boyd   John Ferguson   Claude Dallowe

Edward Evans
James Dewey
James Gevin
Robert Bennet
David Montgomery
William Lowery
Samuel Arsdale
Nathaniel Barret

George Gibbons
Jacob Myer
Fredk. Rupart
Henry Ernest
Alexander Pierry
Thomas Burk
Adam Leonard
Hugh Stone

Christopher Helsley
John Beyans
Thomas Burris
John Farmer
Philip Walters
Robert Bennet

Left with the Wounded.

Michael Walker
William Broughton

Henry Bristwoe
Mark Hollis

Wounded.

Robert Stewart
Tim. Conway

William Gardne
Joshua Jordan

Killed.

Barnaby McKan

William Pullen

Lame on the Road.

John May
John Gallohour
John Clements

John Huston
William McIntire

Missing.

John Bisnor
William Holland

Mathew Howard

Sick in the Camp.

Hugh McKay

James Daily

Taken Prisoner.

Jacob Arrens

Absent on Leave.

John McGuire
   (Signed) G. Mercer.
   Source: Force MSS., Library of Congress.

This pay roll of the Virginia Regiment is preserved among the Washington papers in the Department of State at Washington.

PAY ROLL OF THE VIRGINIA REGIMENT.

Commencing from the 29th of May and ending July 29th, 1754.
Of the Commissioned Officers.   Sum Paid
Colonel, - - - - - - - - - - -   £45.
Lieut.-Col. George Muse till the 20th of July, - - - -   31.15.0
Lieut. Adam Stephen from the 20th of July with his other pay
   as Major and Captain, - . - - - - -   31. 0.6
Major Robert Stobo, his pay as Captain and Major from the
   20th of July, - - - - - - - - -   25. 6.0
Captain Peter Hog, - - - - - - - - -   24. 8.0
Captain Andrew Lewis, - - - - - - - - -   24. 8.0

Captain Jacob Vanbraam, - - - - - - - -	£24. 8.0
Captain George Mercer, - - - - - - - -	23.12.0
Captain Thomas Waggoner, - - - - - - -	14. 0.0
Captain William Polson, - - - - - - -	13.12.0
Lieut. John Savage, - - - - - - - -	12. 4.0
Lieut. James Towers, - - - - - - - -	12. 2.0
Lieut. William Bronaugh, - - - - - - -	9.12.0
Lieut. John Mercer, - - - - - - - -	9.11.0
Lieut. James Craik, - - - - - - - -	9.10.0
Lieut. John West, - - - - - - - - -	12. 4.0
Ensign William Wright from 20th July, - - - -	
Ensign Carolus Sprittdolph from 21st July, - - - -	1. 4.0
Ensign Thomas Bullett from 23rd July, - - - -	1. 1.0
Ensign Walter Stuart from 23rd July (mistake in ye date), -	
Major John Carlyle, Commissary of Stores, etc., - - - -	32. 0.6
Mr. Peyrouney (Ensign and Adjutant) from 3rd June, - -	20. 7.0
Mr. Craik, Surgeon, as ditto, - - - - - -	12. 4.0
Sum pd. ye several Officers, - - - -	£389. 9.0

PAY ROLL OF CAPTAIN ROBERT STOBO'S COMPANY.

Thomas Langdon, Serjeant, - - - - - - -	£4.11.6
Robert Tunstall, Serjeant, - - - - - - -	4.11.6
Nathan Lewis, Corporal, - - - - - - -	3. 1.0
James Carson, Drummer, - - - - - - -	3. 1.0

The following named privates each received £2.0.8 :

John Jones	Jesse Morris	Henry Bowman
John Goldson	James Welsh	John Harwood
Joseph Gibbs	Solomon Batson	James Milton
Adam Jones	Charles Waddey	William Swallow
Richard Smith	Henry Neale	Thomas Ogden
Henry Bailey	Robert McCoy	Michael McGaugh
Benjamin Gause	John Brown	Peregrine Williams
Jacob Going	Joseph Casterson	Anthony Canaday
William Stallions	Alexander Stewart	John Carroll
John Capshaw	Patrick Doughy	James Good

PAY ROLL OF CAPT. PETER HOG'S COMPANY.

Edmond Waggoner, Serjeant, - - - - - - -	£4.11.6
Richard Trotter, Serjeant, - - - - - - -	4.11.6
James Thomas, Corporal, - - - - - - -	3. 1.0
Nicholas Morgan, Corporal, - - - - - - -	3. 1.0

The following named privates each received £2.0.8 :

James Samuel	Joshua Burton	Samuel Hayden
Robert Jones	John Ogleby	Zachary Smith
Joseph Milton	Southy Hayslap	Thomas Nap
Benjamin Hamilton	Argyle House	Bibby Brooks
Joseph Scott	Andrew Clark	Thomas Slaughter
Philip Gatewood	Charles Jones	Joseph Gatewood
Matthew Cox	Peter Afflack	Bryant Page

John Martin	Marshall Pratt	John Chapman
James Hyler	William Dean	Matthew Levison
Michael Scully	Duncan Ferguson	William Underhill
Matthew Durham	David Gorman	Edward Goodwin
William Johnston	Thomas Chaddock	James Megs
William Coleman	John Ramsay	Thomas Harris
Abner Hayslap	Andrew Fowler	John Mears
Thomas Moss	Robert Elliott	James Letort
	Thomas Cellars	

PAY ROLL OF CAPTAIN ANDREW LEWIS' COMPANY.

John McCully, Serjeant, - - - - - - - - £4.11.6
Abraham Mashaw, Drummer, - - - - - - - 3. 1.0

The following named privates each received £2.0.8 :

Robert Graham	Tames Titus	Thomas Pearson
Josias Baker	Nathan Chapman	Michael McCannon
John Marston	John Biddlecomb	James Ludlow
Terence Swinney	Patrick McPike	John Fields
Thomas Stedman	John Mulholland	John Burk
John Smith	Cornelius Henley	Bartholomew Barnes
Matthew Jones	John Triston	John Durham
James Fulham	Thomas Burney	John Roe
	Robert Murphew	

PAY ROLL OF CAPTAIN VAN BRAAM'S COMPANY.

John Hamilton, Serjeant-Major, - - - - - - - £4.11.6
Rodolph Brickner, Serjeant, - - - - - - - - 4.11.6
Thomas Carter, Serjeant, - - - - - - - - 4.11.6
Nicholas Major, Corporal, - - - - - - - - 3. 1.0
John Allan, Corporal, - - - - - - - - - 3. 1.0
Ezekiel Richardson, Drummer, - - - - - - - 3. 1.0

The following named privates each received £2.0.8 :

John Johnston	John Thompson	Thoms Donnahough
William Mitchell	Francis Rogers	Michael Franks
John Stuart	Benjamin Spicer	Francis Self
John McGregory	Edward Whitehead	William Carter
William Knowles	Hugh Paul	Richard Bolton
Charles Allbury	Angus McDonald	Robert Bell
John Campbell	Arthur Howard	Wile Johnson
Edward King	Joseph Powel	John Coin
James Black	Dempsey Simonds	William Gerrard
Patrick Galloway	John Potter	George Taylor
	William Hogan	

PAY ROLL OF CAPTAIN GEORGE MERCER'S COMPANY.

Mark Hollis, Serjeant, - - - - - - - - - £4.11.6
James Tyrroll, Serjeant, - - - - - - - - 4.11.6
Hugh McCoy, Corporal, - - - - - - - - - 3. 1.0
John Boydd, Corporal, - - - - - - - - - 3. 1.0
Edward Evans, Drummer, - - - - - - - - 3. 1.0

The following named privates each received £2.0.8 :

James Dailey	George Gibbons	John McQuire
Robert Bennett	Hugh Stone	William Broughton
Philip Waters	Alexander Perry	Thomas Burris
William Holland	John Farmer	John Gallihour
David Montgomery	Henry Bristow	John May
William Lowery	Claud Dallow	Richard Prichard
Samuel Arsdale	James Ford	Christopher Bombgardner
Nathaniel Barrett	James Cammock	Henry Earnest
John Ferguson	John Clements	Fredk. Rupart

Enlisted Per Lieut. West.

Hugh Ratchford	George Malcomb
Jasper Moorhead	Bryan Conner
William Tyan	Timothy Conway

The following list of officers and men of the Virginia Regt. is taken from a pay bill of a detachment sent to Augusta County under the command of Captain Andrew Lewis, commencing the 29th of July and ending the 29th of Sept., 1754 :

Andrew Lewis, Captain	Robert Graham, Serjeant
John Savage, Lieutenant	Thomas Stedman, Corporal
William Wright, Ensign	Joshua Baker, Corporal
John McKully, Serjeant	David Wilkinson, Drummer

Privates.

Abraham Mushaw	Charles Waddey	John Gallihon
John Biddlecomb	James Smith	Casper Moreau
Robert Murphy	William Stallions	John Chapman
Barth. Burns	Henry Bowman	Samuel Hyden
James Fulham	James Milton	William Dean
John Thurstan	Jacob Gowen	Nicholas Morgan
Thomas Burney	Henry Bailey	Barnaby Ryley
John Maston	John Brown	Nathl. Deadman
Terrence Swiney	Henry Neale	Andrew Fowler
John Smith	Benjamin Gauze	John Allan
Patrick Smith	John Hart	(till this a Corporal)
John Mulholland	George Gibbons	Thomas King (discharged)
James Cammock	William Holland	William Chaplain
Patrick McPike	Thomas Burras	John Davis
Michael McCannon	Samuel Arsdale	John Campbell
Matthew Jones	George Malcom	Francis Rogers
Thomas Pierce	Philemon Waters	Pledge Ward
	James Ford	

MEMBERS OF THE VIRGINIA REGIMENT WHO HAVE RECEIVED BOUNTY MONEY.

The following lists are preserved in the "Force Manuscripts" in the Library of Congress. On the back of each of the five rolls is the indorsement of Washington.

A List of Captain Stobo's Company, Who Have Received His Excellency's Bounty Money.

Henry Bailey	James Good	Richard Morris
Solomon Batson	Edward Graves	Henry Neil
Henry Bowman	John Harwood	Thomas Ogden
John Brown	Adam Jones	Charles Smith
John Carroll	John Jones	Richard Smith
James Carson, drummer	Anthony Kennedy	William Stallions
Joseph Casterton	Thomas Langden, Serj.	Alexander Stewart
Patrick Duphy	Nathan Lewis, Corporal	William Swallow
Nicholas Foster	Michael McGroth	Robert Tunstall, Serjeant
Benj. Gause	Robert McKay	Charles Waddey
Joseph Gibbs	James Milton	James Welch
Jacob Going	Jessy Morris	Peregrine Williams
John Golson		

A List of Captain Hogg's Company Who Have Received His Excellency's Bounty Money.

Bibby Brooks	Benj. Hamilton	Nicholas Morgan
Joshua Burton	Abner Haslip	Thomas Moss
Thomas Chaddock	Southy Haslip	Thomas Napp
John Chapman	James Hyler	John Ogilby
Andrew Clark	William Hogan	Byron Page
William Coleman	Angoile House	Marshall Pratt
Mathew Cox	Samuel Hyden	John Ramsay
William Dean	Charles Joames	John Roe
Mathew Durham	William Johnston	James Samuel
Robert Ellot	Robert Jones	Joseph Scott
Peter Essleet	James Letort	Michael Scully
Duncan Ferguson	Mathew Levison	Dudley Skinner
James Ford	—— McGuire	Thomas Slaughter
Andrew Fowler	John Martin	Zach. Smith
Joseph Gatewood	John Mears	James Thomas
Philip Gatewood	James Meggs	Richard Trotter, Serjeant
Edward Goodwin	Joseph Milton	William Underhill
David Gorman	Dominick Moran	Edmund Waggoner, Serj.

A List of Captain Lewis's Company Who Have Received His Excellency's Bounty Money.

Josias Baker, Corporal
Joseph Baxter
John Biddlecom
Daniel Billot
John Burk
Bartholomew Burns
Thomas Burney
Edward Cahill
William Cairns
James Cammack
Nathl. Chapman
Patrick Coyl
John Durham
John Featon

James Ferguson
John Field
James Fullham
Robert Grimes, Serjeant
Cornelius Handly
William Harbinson
Matthew Jones
James Ludlow
Michael McCannon
John McCully, Serjeant
Patrick McPike
John Maston
John Mulholland
Robert Murphy
Abraham Mushaw

John Poor
William Poor
James Price
John Rowe
John Smith
John Smith
George Swiney
Terence Swiney
James Titus
Elijah Ward
Arthur Watts
Thomas Wedman, Corp.
John Whitman
Daniel Wilkinson

A List of Captain Van Braam's Company Who Have Received His Excellency's Bounty Money.

John Allan, Corporal
Charles Allbury
Robert Bell
James Balck
Richard Bolton
Godfrey Bomgardner
Rudolph Brickner
Christopher Byerly
John Campbell
Thomas Carter, Serjeant
William Carter
Mathew Chape
John Coin
Thomas Donahough
Bernard Draxter

Michael Franks
Patrick Gallaway
William Gerrard
George Gobell
John Hamilton
  Sergeant-Major
Thomas Hennesey
Arthur Howard
John Johnston
Wile Johnston
Edward King
William Knowles
John Lee
Angus McDonald
John Mackgrigory
Edward Whitehead

Nicholas Major
George Markham
Edward Minor
William Mitchell
Hugh Paul
John Potter
Joseph Powell
Ezekiel Richardson
Francis Rogers
Francis Self
Dernsey Simons
Benjamin Spicer
John Steuart
George Taylor
John Thornton

A List of Captain Mercer's Company, Who Have Received His Excellency's Bounty Money.

Samuel Arsdale
Nath. Barret
Robert Bennett
John Bishop
Charles Bombgardner
John Boyd
Henry Bristowe
William Broughton

Henry Earnest
Edward Evans
John Farmer
John Ferguson
James Ford
John Gallahour
Christopher Haltzley
William Holland

John McQuire
John Maid
John May
David Montgomerie
Jacob Myer
Alexander Perry
Ritchard Pritchard
Frederick Rupard

Thomas Burk	Mark Hollis, Serjeant	Mathew Stanard
Thomas Burris	Adam Leonard	Hugh Stone
John Clements	William Lowrey	James Tyrrall, Serjeant
Timothy Conway	William McIntire	Michael Walker
James Daly	Hugh McKoy	Philip Walters
Claud Dallowe		

LIST OF OFFICERS OF THE VIRGINIA REGIMENT CONTAINED IN THE JOURNAL OF CAPTAIN CHARLES LEWIS.

Expedition Against the French Oct. 10—Dec. 27, 1755.

The Hon. Geo. Washington
Lt. Col. Adam Stevens
Major Andrew Lewis.

Captains.

Peter Hogg	Wm. Branough	Carter Harrison
Geo. Mercer	John Mercer	Charles Lewis
Thos. Waggoner	Joshua Lewis	Wm. Peachy
Robt. Stewart	Hy. Woodward	David Bell
Thos. Cock	Robt. Spotswood	Robert McKenzie
Jno. Savage		

Lieutenants.

John McNiel	Geo. Frazer	Jno. Campbell
Wm. Stark	John Edward Lomax	John Hall
Thos. Bullett	Peter Steenburger	John Lowry
Walter Stewart	Jno. Williams	John King
John Blagg	Augustine	James Baker
Hancock Eustice	Brockenborough	

Ensigns.

Mordecai Buckner	Nathl. Milner	Charles Smith
John Polson	Wm. Flemming	Lee Hussis Dekizer
Wm. Dangerfield	Leonard Price	Geo. Gordon
Edwd. Hubbard	Nathl. Thompson	Geo. Weeden
Jno. Dean	Thos. Carter	

Source: Va. Hist. Coll.; Vol. XI, p. 213.

VIRGINIA OFFICERS AT BRADDOCK'S DEFEAT, 1755.

(K. Killed). (W. Wounded).

Captain Stevens (W)	Captain Stewart	Lieut. Spiltdorph (K)
Captain Peyronie	Lieut. Hamilton (K)	Lieut. Stewart (W)
Captain Waggoner	Lieut. Woodward	Lieut. Waggener (K)
Captain Polson (K)	Lieut. Wright (K)	Lieut. McNeill

Source: Gentlemen's Magazine, Aug., 1755.

To Geo. Washington, Esq., Col. of the Va. Regt. and Commander of all the Va. Forces:

The humble Address of the officers of the Va. Regt. (Signed).

Geo. Weedon	Wm. Cocke	Thos. Bullitt
Hy. Russell	David Kennedy	Jno. Blagg
Jno. Lawson	Jas. Craik, Surgeon	Natha. Gist
Geo. Speak	James Duncanson	Mord. Buckner
Wm. Woodford	Jas. Roy	Wm. Dangerfield
Jno. McCully	Robt. Stewart	Wm. Fleming
Jno. Sallard	Jno. McNeill	Leonard Price
W. Hughes	H. Woodward	Nathl. Thompson
Walt. Cunningham	Robt. McKenzie	Chas. Smith

Fort Loudoun, Dec. 31, 1758.

An address on his retirement as Commander of the Va. troops, 27 Dec. 1758.

Source : Records of Columbia Hist. Soc., Vol. I, p. 24.

Spotsylvania Order Books.

A list of the officers of the Colonial Militia of Spotsylvania County who producing their commissions before the Court of His Majesty's Honourable Justices for the County aforesaid, took the oaths as directed by law.

ORDER BOOK—1724-1730.

Colonel John Robinson took the oath as Lieutenant of Spots. Co., August 5, 1729.

Captain Thomas Chew and his officers, John Minor and Edward Franklyn; Captain William Johnson and his officers, Andrew Harrison and Thomas Warren, took ye oath August 5, 1729.

Major Goodrich Lightfoot, Captain Robert Slaughter and his officers, Francis Kirkley and William Payton; Captain John Scott and his officers, Joseph Hawkins and John Lightfoot; Captain William Bledsoe and his officers, James Williams and George Home, took ye oath, September 2, 1729.

Captain William Hansford and his officer, John Grayson, Jr., took ye oath, October 7, 1729.

Henry Willis, Gent., before His Honor, William Gooch, Esq., Lt.-Gov., etc. Commission to be Lieut.-Colonel of this county, took ye oath, August 4, 1730.

ORDER BOOK—1730-1738.

Robert Green, Captain; Francis Slaughter, Lieut.; John Roberts, Ensign; Abraham Field, Captain; Henry Field, Lieut.; Francis Michall, Ensign of a company of foot, took the oath February 2, 1730-1.

Benjamin Cave, Lieutenant to Captain John Scott, took the oath, February 2, 1730-1.

John Taliaferro, Lieut.-Colonel; Francis Thornton, Jr., Major of the Horse; Francis Taliaferro, Captain of the Horse; Richard Tutt, his Lieutenant of Horse; Thomas Hill, Captain of a foot company, took ye oath, October 6, 1736.

Richard Phillips, Gent., Lieutenant, and Edward Herndon, Jr., Gent., Cornet, produced their commissions and took the oath, etc., as officers to a troop of horse under Captain William Waller. November 1, 1737.

ORDER BOOK—1738-1749.

Mosely Battaley, Gent., produced his commission to be Captain of a company of Foot in this county, and took the oath Apr., 1740.

Thomas Duerson, Gent., commissioned to be Lieut. and George Green, Gent., commissioned to be Ensign of a company of Foot under Capt. Battaley, and took the oath Apr. 1, 1740.

Francis Thornton, Jr. Gent., commissioned as Lieut.-Colonel of this county; Francis Taliaferro, Gent., commissioned to be Major of the Horse; Richard ——, Gent., commissioned to be Captain of a company of Horse; Rice Curtis, Jr., Gent., commissioned to be captain of a company of Horse; Joseph Hawkins, Gent., commissioned to be captain of a company of Horse. The preceding took the oath Sept. 7, 1742.

Edmund Waller, commissioned to be Captain of a company of Foot; John Edwards, Gent., commissioned to be Captain of a company of Foot; Thomas Duerson, Gent., commissioned to be Captain of a company of Foot. The preceding took the oath Dec. 8, 1742.

William Robinson, Gent., commissioned to be Major of Militia in this county, took the oath Sept. 7, 1743.

Joseph Collins, Gent., commissioned to be Lieutenant of a troop of Horse under Capt. Joseph Hawkins; George Carter, Gent., commissioned to be Cornet under the same. Henry Pendleton, Gent., commissioned to be Lieutenant of a company of Foot, under Capt. Edmund Waller; James Edwards, Gent., commissioned to be Ensign under the same. Dudley Gatewood, Gent., commissioned to be Ensign in a company of Foot, under Capt. Thomas Duerson. The preceding took the oath Dec. 6, 1743.

Henry Brock, Gent., commissioned to be Lieutenant of a company of Foot, under Capt. Thomas Duerson, took the oath Feb. 7, 1743.

John Taliaferro, Gent., commissioned to be captain of a company of Foot, John Gordon, Gent., commissioned to be Lieutenant of a company of Foot, took the oath Dec. 4, 1744.

Edward Herndon, Jr., Gent., commissioned to be Lieutenant of a troop of Horse, commanded by Capt. Richard Tutt, took the oath March 5, 1744.

James Allan, commissioned to be Cornet of a troop of Horse, commanded by Capt. Richard Tutt, took the oath March 6, 1744.

William Waller, Gent., commissioned to be Colonel of the Horse in this county, took the oath July 4, 1749.

John Spotswood, Esq., commission to be Lieut.-Colonel of this county, took the oath Aug. 1, 1749.

ORDER BOOK—1749-1755.

Rice Curtis, Jr., commission to be Major of the Horse; Richard Tutt, Gent., to be Major of the Foot, took the oath Apr. 3, 1750.

Moseley Battaley, Gent., commission to be Captain of a troop of Horse, took the oath Sept. 4, 1750.

Joseph Collins, Gent., commission to be Captain of a company of Foot, took the oath Nov. 6, 1750.

Philemon Hawkins, Gent., commission to be Captain of a company of Foot, took the oath Feb. 5, 1750.

John Spotswood, Esq., commission dated Nov. 18, last, as Lieut. and Chief Commanding Officer of the Militia in this county, took the oath Jan. 3, 1753.

Francis Taliaferro as Colonel in this county; John Thornton as Colonel in this county; Richard Tutt as Major of Militia in this county, produced their commissions, all dated Nov. 18, 1752, and took the oath Feb. 6, 1753.

Wm. Lynn, commission dated Jan. 26, 1753, as Captain of the Independent Company of Foot, composed of the Gentlemen Inhabitants of the Town of Fredericksburg, took the oath Feb. 7, 1753.

John Dent, as Lieutenant and Humphrey Wallace as Ensign to Capt. William Lynn, Gent., Captain of the Independent Company of Foot, dated this day and took ye oath Feb. 7, 1753.

George Washington, Esq., commission dated Dec. 13, 1752, to be Major and Adjutant of the Militia, Horse and Foot, in the counties of Princess Anne, Norfolk, Nansemond, Isle of Wight, Southampton, Surrey, Brunswick, Prince George, Dinwiddie, Chesterfield, Amelia, and Cumberland, and took the oath Feb. 10, 1753.

Charles Lewis, William Miller, and Benjamin Pendleton, Gentlm., commissioned to be Captains of Foot, and Ambrose Bullard to be Lieutenant of Foot, took the oath Sept. 4, 1753.

John Crane, Gent., commission dated Feb. the 11th, last, to be Captain of a troop of Horse, took the oath Nov. 6, 1754.

Abraham Crittenden, William Jesse, Benjamin Whaley, Richard Harkless, James Low, Hugh Carpenter, and John Waller, came into Court and took the oath to the Government, and signed the test, etc., "soldiers," Dec, 3, 1754.

ORDER BOOK—1755-1765.

William Lynn, Gent., Major, commission dated July 29, 1755.

John Dent, Gent., Captain of Fredericksburg Company, commission dated July 22, 1755.

Philemon Hawkins, Gent., Captain of company of Foot, commission dated July 21, 1755.

Bushrod Fauntleroy, Gent., Captain of company of Foot, commission dated July 21, 1755.

Lawrence Taliaferro, Gent., Lieut. of Company under Capt. Charles Lewis, commission dated July 21, 1755.

Moses Bledsoe, Lieutenant of company under Capt. William Miller, commission dated July 27, 1755.

Erasmus Withers Allen, Lieutenant of company under Capt. Philemon Hawkins, commission dated July 21, 1755.

Aaron Bledsoe, Lieutenant of company under Capt. Benjamin Pendleton, commission dated July 21, 1755.

John Herndon, Ensign of company under Capt. Miller, commission dated August 2, 1755.

The preceding took the oath August 5, 1755.

The following officers produced their commissions and took the oath and subscribed the test, as by law directed, at a Court held for Spotsylvania County, May 4, 1756:

Thomas Slaughter, Esq., commission dated Apr. 26, 1756, Lieut.-Colonel and Commander of the Forces from Culpeper against ye Indians above Winchester, on this expedition.

William Green, Gent., as Major under the said Slaughter ; commission dated Apr. 29, 1756.

Francis Kirtley, Gent., Captain of a company of Foot, in the said forces ; commission dated Apr. 29, 1756.

John Field, Gent., Captain of a company of Foot, in the said forces ; commission dated Apr. 29, 1756.

William Stanton, Gent., as 1st Lieutenant in said expedition ; commission dated May 4, 1756.

Lewis Willis, Gent., as Captain of Foot in Spots. County, under John Spotswood, Esq.; commission dated Apr. 29, 1756.

Lawrence Taliaferro, Captain of Foot in Spots. County; commission dated March 4, 1756.

Aaron Bledsoe, Gent., Captain of Foot in Spots. County; commission dated Apr. 29, 1756.

James Cunningham, Gent., as 1st Lieutenant of company of Foot in Spots. County; commission dated May 4, 1756.

William Bell, Gent., 2nd Lieutenant of Foot in Spots. Co.; commission dated May 4, 1756.

Beverley Winslow, Gent., as 1st Lieutenant of Foot in Spots. County; commission dated May 4, 1756.

Robert Chew, Gent., 1st Lieutenant of Foot in Spots. County; commission dated May 4, 1756.

James Tutt, Gent., as 1st Lieutenant of Foot in Spots. County; commission dated May 4, 1756.

Zachary Lewis, Jr., Gent., 1st Lieutenant of Foot in Spots. County; commission dated May 4, 1756.

Edward Herndon, Jr., 2nd Lieutenant of Foot in Spots. County; commission dated May 4, 1756.

Humphrey Brooke, 2nd Lieutenant of Foot in Spots. County; commission dated May 4, 1756.

John Robinson, 2nd Lieutenant of Foot in Spots. County; commission dated May 4, 1756.

Spilsbe Coleman, 2nd Lieutenant of Foot in Spots. County; commission dated May 4, 1756.

The following took the oath at a Court held May 5, 1756:

Benjamin Pendleton, Esq., Major of the Militia in Spots. County; commission dated Apr. 29, 1756.

William Taliaferro, Esq., Lieut.-Colonel of Orange County; commission dated May 4, 1756.

Thomas Estes, as Ensign to Capt. Fauntleroy; commission dated July 21, 1755.

John Waller, the Younger, Gent., commission to be Lieutenant of a troop of Horse in Spots. County, dated July 21, 1755; took the oath July 6, 1756.

Rice Curtis, Gent., commission as Colonel of Militia of Spots. County, dated Apr. 26, 1756; took the oath July 7, 1756.

Thomas Estes, Gent., commission to be Captain of a company of Foot in this county; dated March 11, 1757, and John Herndon commission to be Ensign of a company of Foot; took the oath Apr. 5, 1757.

Charles Lewis, Gent., Major of the County of Spots.; commission dated Oct. 4, 1757; took the oath Oct. 4, 1757.

Richard Tutt, Colonel in the Militia of Spots. Co.; commission dated Aug. 27, 1756; took the oath Oct. 4, 1757.

Fielding Lewis, Esq., County Lieutenant of Spots. County; commission dated Oct. 15; took the oath Feb, 7, 1758,

Zachary Lewis, Jr., Gent., Captain of company of Foot in Spots. County; commission dated Feb. 17, 1758.

George Frazer, Gent., Captain of company of Foot; commission dated March 8, 1758.

Robt. Duncanson, Gent., to be Lieutenant.

Hugh Lenox, Gent., to be Ensign.

The above took the oaths March 8, 1758.

Joseph Brock, Gent., commission dated Oct. 25, 1758, to be Captain of a company in this County.

Zachary Lewis, Gent., commissson dated Oct. 23, 1758, to be Captain of a company in this County.

John Crane, Gent., commission dated Oct. 25, 1758, to be Major in this County.

John Carter, Gent., commission dated Oct. 25, 1758; to be Captain of a company in this County.

The preceding took the oaths Apr. 3, 1759.

Joseph Bledsoe, Gent., commission dated Apr. 8, 1759, to be Ensign of a company in the 14th Battalion; took the oath May 1, 1759.

Fielding Lewis, Esq., commission dated Oct. 25, 1758, to be County Lieutenant.

Beverley Winslow, Gent., commission dated Oct. 25, 1758, to be Captain of a company of Militia in this County.

The above took the oaths June 4, 1759.

Fielding Lewis, Esq., commission dated Nov. 12, 1761, as Commander in Chief of the Militia of this County.

John Crane, Gent., commission dated Nov. 12, 1761, to be Major of the Militia in this County.

Joseph Brock, commission dated Nov. 12, 1761, to be Captain of a company in this County.

The above took the oaths March 1, 1762.

Zachary Lewis, Gent., commission dated Nov. 12, 1761, to be Captain of a company in this County; took the oath Apr. 5, 1762.

John Waller, Esq., commission dated Apr. 4, 1764, to be Captain of a company of Foot.

John Beverley Roy, Gent., commission dated May 7, 1764, as a Lieutenant of a company of Foot.

The above took the oaths May 7, 1764.

John Lewis, Esq., commission to be Quarter Master of the Militia in this County; took the oath Aug. 1, 1763.

John Waller, Gent., commission dated July 11, 1763, to be Lieutenant of a company of Militia.

James Cunningham, commission dated July 27, 1763, to be Lieutenant of a company of Militia.

The above took the oaths Aug. 1, 1763.

George Weeden, Esq., commission dated March 1, 1764, to be Captain of a company of Militia; took the oath March 5, 1764.

Zachary Lewis, Jr., Esq., commission dated Apr. 30, 1764, to be Major in the Militia; took the oath Aug. 7, 1764.

Robert Chew, Esq., commission dated Sept. 3, 1764, to be Captain of a company of Militia; took the oath Sept. 4, 1764.

John Crane, Esq., commission dated Apr. 3, 1764, to be Colonel in the Militia in this County.

John Roan, commission dated March 5, 1765, to be Captain of a company of Militia.

The above took the oaths Apr. 2, 1765.

James Cunningham, commission dated Sept. 2, 1755, Ensign to Capt. Benjamin Pendleton; took the oath Sept. 3, 1755.

George Frazer, Gent., commission dated Aug. 23, 1755, as Lieutenant of a company in the Virginia Regiment; took the oath Dec. 4, 1755.

ORDER BOOK—1768-1774.

George Stubblefield, Gent., commission dated May 9, 1769, Capt. of a company of Mititia; took the oath Nov. 6, 1769.

Henry Johnson, Gent., commission dated May 9, 1769, Lieutenant in the Militia of Spots. Co.; took the oath Nov. 6, 1769.

ORDER BOOK—1774-1782.

The following proved their right to bounty lands granted by His Majesty the King to soldiers serving in defense of the Colony 1755 to 1760, etc.:

Thomas Collins, Decd., Sergt. and Capt. in Capt. Charles Lewis' company of a Virginia Regiment on the frontier, 1755; proved at a Court held for Spots. County, Sept. 16, 1779.

Richard Johnston, Lieutenant in Col. William Byrd's Regiment in Cherokee Expedition in 1760.

Edward Ludwick (Ludwig or Ledwedge) served as a soldier in 1st Virginia Regiment, raised for the immediate defense of the Colony in 1756.

James Richards, served as a soldier in 1st Virginia Regiment, raised for immediate defense of the Colony in 1760.

Ezekiel Richardson served as Drum Major 1st Virginia Regiment, raised for immediate defense of the Colony, in 1758, also served as Drum Major in Regiment under command of Col. Adam Stephen in the year 1760.

Stephen Spicer, served as a soldier in the year 1758.

The above proved their services at a Court held for Spots. County, Apr. 21, 1780.

George Stubblefield, Gent., served as a Cadet in the year 1762, in Regiment under the command of Adam Stephen.

Proved at a Court held for Spots. County, June 15, 1780.

At a Court held for Spots. County, February, 1780, the following proved their services in the Militia of the Colony, 1755 to 1760, raised for the immediate defense thereof:

Edward Foley served as a soldier in 1st Va. Regiment.

Edward Sutton, soldier.

William Ross, soldier.

Charles —— as Sergt.

William Tins —— as soldier.

William Lampton as soldier.

Daniel Simpson as Corp.

Edward Gold —— as Ensign in Col. Byrd's Regiment.

Nathaniel Gest (or Gist) deposeth and saith that he served in the office of Lieut. in Capt. Christopher Gest's company, raised in 1756, and served until the company was —— and also as a Captain in Col. George Washington's 1st Va. Regiment, raised in 1756, ——— continued as Captain until it was disbanded.

Nathaniel Gest, son and heir of Christopher Gest, decd., deposeth and saith that the said Christopher Gest was Captain of a Company of Rangers, raised in 1756, for defense of the frontier, and served until the said company was discharged in 1756.

Genl. George Weeden served as a Capt.-Lieut. in 1st Va. Regiment; also served as Captain in Col. Adam Stephen's Regiment.

Larkin Chew served as Ensign in Col. William Byrd's 2nd Va. Regiment, raised in 1758; served until disbanded, and also served in 1st Va. Regiment as a Lieut., at that time under command of Col. Byrd, served therein until it was disbanded. Afterwards entered regiment commanded by Col. Adam Stephen and served as Lieutenant until it was disbanded.

William Dangerfield served as Captain in 1st Va. Regiment till disbanded, afterwards in regiment commanded by Col. Adam Stephen.

Richard Halbe——, soldier in Col. Byrd's and Col. Stephen's regiments.

Robert Saunders, Corp. in Frontier Battalion,

James Gimb——, as soldier in Col. Byrd's regiment.

John Conner as soldier in Col. Stephen's regiment.

Richard Br——, Serg. in Col. Byrd's Regiment, 1758.

Ludowick Oneal, as soldier in Col. Byrd's Regiment, 1758.

Joseph ——, Serg. 2nd Va. Regiment in 1758.

Richard F. A——, as soldier.

Francis ——, as soldier.

William Tur ——, as soldier in Byrd's Regiment.

Richard Reynolds, soldier in Byrd's Regiment.

Benjamin Turner, decd., soldier in Byrd's Regiment.

Joseph Bledsoe, Serg. in —— Va. Regiment, also served as Ensign in the ——er Battalion.

Index of Counties.

General Index.

CPSIA information can be obtained
at www.ICGtesting.com
Printed in the USA
LVOW03s0508041017
551023LV00006B/67/P